Philanthropists, Therapists and Activists

Philanthropists, Therapists and Activists

A Century of Ideological Conflict in Social Work

Gerald C. Rothman

SCHENKMAN PUBLISHING COMPANY, INC.
Cambridge, Massachusetts

Copyright © 1985
Schenkman Publishing Company, Inc.
190 Concord Avenue
Cambridge, MA 02138

Library of Congress Cataloging in Publication Data

Rothman, Gerald C.
  Philanthropists, therapists, and activists.

  Bibliography: p.
  Includes index.
    1. Social service—United States—History.   2. Social
work education—United States—History.   3. Social
workers—United States—History.   I. Title.
HV91.R745   1985   361.3′0973   84-23514
ISBN 0-87073-521-7
ISBN 0-87073-524-1 (pbk.)

Printed in the United States of America.

DEDICATION
To Sue, Eli, and Miriam

Table of Contents

Acknowledgments

It is difficult to acknowledge all of the people whose knowledge and assistance resulted in my being able to complete this work. I am, however, particularly indebted to my friends and colleagues Fred Muskal and John Erlich whose consistent help played a major role in encouraging me to continue my efforts over the years. Thanks are also due to Herb Kutchins and Anthony Platt for their support and insights as the book was being planned and written. I am also grateful to Norine Maisler and Fay Goleman who shared their libraries with me and inspired the initiation of this work. Finally, I am most indebted to my wife, Sue, without whose patience, encouragement and hours of editing and proofreading this work would not have been accomplished.

Introduction

Histories of the field of social work often tend to picture the development of the profession as an outgrowth of a single ideology. A closer examination, however, reveals quite a different picture. Although often obscured by controversy about technique or curriculum at schools of social work, there exists an ongoing debate about the ideology of the profession. This conflict centers around the appropriate arena for social work practice.

For more than a century the profession has agonized, theorized and compromised about whether its helping role should be rooted in a model of individual counseling or in activism to promote client well-being through social change.

The implied ideology of the activist stance is one of redistribution of societal resources in the interest of equity. The counseling position, although claiming to support activism in spirit, operates apolitically in practice. In reality this noninvolvement represents a conservative ideology of support of the status quo. The inability of the profession to resolve this basic issue has resulted in inconsistencies in the posture of the profession relative to issues central to its practice.

This inconsistency is reflected in the public image of social work. The profession has been identified, credited and discredited as the supporter of liberal causes. On the one hand social workers are vilified as "bleeding hearts" by conservative elements of society, overidentified with deviant populations and viewed as unwilling to take the necessary steps to correct wrong-doing. On the other hand, the profession is often seen by poor and oppressed people and their advocates as incompetent, at best, with skills irrelevant to their needs. At worst, social workers are viewed by these people as the agents of a societal system that seeks to subjugate the clients they claim to serve.

As the profession has sought to define its theories, methods, and goals, it has been able to do so only in the broadest and most general terms. As is true in other professions, social work seeks to help people with personal and social problems. The failure to come to grips with the basic ideological stance of social work practice, however, results in difficulty in reaching greater specificity. The effect of this is not only confusion but ongoing debate about the definition of basic areas that are critical to the profession. This debate has been recurrent and has been characterized by an inability or unwillingness to resolve the most fundamental issues. Thus these same issues arise repeatedly. They are addressed partially, submerged for a time, and present themselves again at times of crisis or other social change. Such areas include the ethics of practice, the major theoretical framework from which it operates, the necessary qualifications and education for the professional, and the demeanor and character expected of the practitioner. Also included, as mentioned above, is a lack of definition of the appropriate methods for practice. What becomes clear is that the problems in the different areas are problems of the total profession that are reflected in its component parts.

This interrelatedness is reflected in the subject areas defined in social work education. Recent tradition has divided these areas into social work practice, human behavior in the social environment (or theoretical foundations of practice), history and philosophy of social work and social welfare (often called "Policy"), and research and field practice. Trends in the profession are of vital importance in the content of each of the different areas. For example, the domination of the field by the counseling perspective has resulted in human behavior courses stressing theories that are psychological rather than sociological in nature. Policy courses tend to be chronological, biographical and descriptive rather than analytical. Mention of Marxism, socialism or even social conflict in texts and course outlines is almost always minimal or absent. The content of field experience is aimed at creating basic learning. This becomes defined as "direct practice" or casework. There are few opportunities for field placements that emphasize activism, planning and administration that are offered in the curriculum. Also minimized is research which often narrowly confines itself to counseling issues, tends to be regarded with trepidation by students who look upon it as irrelevant to practice and tolerated by faculty as a necessary evil.

Through one hundred years of history the profession has been dominated by caseworkers. They originated an agency known as the Charity Organization Society. This agency was devoted to the distribution of funds made available by philanthropists. It sought to make efficient use of available resources, determine eligibility, and help the poor correct behavior that bound them to poverty.

Another group of social workers was more devoted to social reform. Their initial strongholds were agencies called settlement houses. These people sought to share the life experiences of the poor by residing in their communities and to build a relationship based on familiarity. A sharing of culture would then become possible along with the development of a community organization that would hopefully result in political reform that would serve the public good.

In spite of the influence of the Charity Organization Society, there have been times when social reform was called for. This was particularly true during the Great Depression. In such periods the charity people (who later became the "therapy" people) allowed the field to be represented by the reformers. In the Franklin Roosevelt administration these reformers played a major role in forming social policy. When this happened the therapists retained control of professional schools and prestigious private agencies but remained in the background insofar as public policy was concerned. They did, however, maintain the stance of the agencies and curriculum of the schools in the same casework mold as before.

Periods of social reform come and go. When support for social workers as reformers declined, so did the values and goals of reform, since they had not been institutionalized in the educational process. The field, therefore, retained the conservative charity organization perspective that had become the mainstay of the schools of social work. The character of the current profession of social work is a direct reflection of these events. Social work is now overwhelmingly a counseling profession. Practice in the social reform arena is a remnant of what it was and has not been truly functional since the Depression years. The profession has, therefore, been unable to lead social change even during times of crisis when the opportunity to do so presented itself during the activist years of the 1960s and 1970s. Today the value of the profession has been questioned from many quarters, accounting for a defensive stance and a sense of vulnerability during the years of retrenchment in the 1980s. We will attempt to present an analysis of the past activities of social work in the hope that it will point the direction for the profession to follow in order to survive the current economic crisis, while maintaining ideological integrity. This is done in the hope that not only will the profession survive, but will also contribute to American life in a meaningful way.

Summary

Philanthropists, Therapists and Activists first looks at the historical background that set the stage for the formation of schools of social work during the years of 1895 to 1917. Two major conflicts that occurred as the schools were being formed in the first decade of the twentieth century are then examined. The first of these was the debate over the knowledge base of the new profession. The second controversy dealt with the affiliation of professional schools of social work with established universities. The book then deals with the image of the ideal social worker as manifested in entry requirements to the profession and admission requirements to schools. Next we look at the effects of the conflict and its resolution in the social work education curriculum. The book's final section is an examination of the outcome of established educational practices in the schools upon the profession after 1930.

Chapter 1

The Current Crisis in Social Work and its Roots: An Overview

The current political era is one of retrenchment in social programs including those concerned with welfare and education. Programs put in place during the administration of Franklin Roosevelt and enhanced by following administrations through Richard Nixon are now being financially crippled and dismantled. These programs, according to proponents of the current trend, are wasteful, in no way accomplish the goals they were designed to accomplish, and encourage malingering and fraud by those who are dependent upon them. There has even been the assertion at the highest level of government that the social problems that the programs are designed to ameliorate—such as poverty—cannot even be proven to exist in the United States and that those who take advantage of food programs do so because they are unwilling to cook for themselves.

Although there always was conservative opposition to such programs, they came to be accepted in the mainstream of American politics. Republican as well as Democratic political leaders claimed to support them in theory, if not in fact. President Eisenhower boasted of bipartisan support of the Social Security program and did little to change existing programs. Richard Nixon suggested far-reaching welfare reforms that included a guaranteed minimum income (Leiby, pp. 326–327). To those engaged in the administration of social programs it seemed that the basic assumptions underlying their services had become institutionalized.

Gradually the general acceptance of programs began to be eroded. While Presidents Kennedy and Johnson sought to vastly expand welfare programs, a counter movement of cutbacks developed in some state programs. In the early sixties, the city of Newburgh, New York, initiated punitive welfare policies. In Ohio, at about the same time,

Governor James Rhodes initiated a reversal in welfare policy. This involved reductions in grants, more severe means testing and the imposition of widespread work projects to discourage assumed malingering of welfare recipients.

Ronald Reagan, then governor of California, provided another example. He built his political career on the notion of "welfare reform." His program was built on the widely held but untrue beliefs that assistance programs were rife with fraud, providing recipients with a standard of living beyond that of working people, and supporting those who were able but unwilling to work. Like Rhodes, Reagan's "reform" restated the existing punitive aspects of assistance laws. In addition, he expanded many of the restrictive aspects of the programs and introduced new ones. He also attacked many other government programs, cutting back such areas as health, mental health and education (Kerby, pp. 262–267). Ultimately most of the "reforms" proved to be unworkable or were found to be illegal by the courts. Whatever savings accrued to the state were not reimbursed to taxpayers. Instead, huge unused surpluses in state income began accumulating. Nonetheless, in spite of the absence of real success, Reagan and his programs gained enormous popularity which eventually helped to propel him into the presidency.

The effective vote-getting tactics of the cutback approach attracted many imitators. Within the Republican Party the position became more respectable as the mainstream and less confined to its conservative right wing. Jerry Brown, Reagan's Democratic successor as governor of California, sought to capitalize on the apparent popularity of governmental parsimony. Borrowing a page from conservative ideology, he attacked "big government" rather than specific beneficiary groups (Martz, p. 23). This he combined with notions from environmentalism and Zen popular with his intellectual supporters to produce a philosophical base from which to launch a cutback program of his own. He argued that past administrations had not taken into account limited resources. Government spending had depleted finances and it was now necessary to conserve what was left. Rather than respond to needs it was now necessary for government to lower its expectations of what could be accomplished.

Brown shared Reagan's failure and success. While he continued the program-demolition begun by Reagan, he was unable to pass on savings to taxpayers. Unused state surpluses continued to accumulate at an even faster pace. Brown gained national prominence. He ran an unsuccessful but surprisingly strong campaign for the Democratic presidential nomination in 1976 and a successful reelection campaign for the California governorship in 1978. Unlike Reagan, Brown was unable to disguise or otherwise render acceptable his ineptitude and opportunism. His popularity waned and he was soundly defeated in a bid to represent California in the United States Senate in 1982. Although he is not a potent political force in California politics at this time, Brown is still viewed by some as having political potential.

What Jerry Brown did accomplish was further legitimation of the politics of retrenchment. In California the public was convinced that severe cuts in taxation would not affect programs of value. The huge surpluses in state funds supported the idea that monies raised by taxes were not truly needed. Therefore, an initiative that, in similar form, had been previously defeated and opposed as destructive to the operation of government by Ronald Reagan, passed as Proposition Thirteen. Similar initiatives were subsequently seen in many states.

In addition, Brown's position gave cutbacks in social programs greater bipartisan acceptability than they had previously enjoyed. It was apparently an enormously popular stand which would appeal to many voters. It was adopted by the Carter administration and, following the Reagan presidential election in 1980, spawned a significant Democratic movement called "Neo-Liberalism." What had been an unacceptably reactionary view of social programs seems to have become the accepted stand of mainstream American politics.

Popularity for retrenchment arose from a number of social and economic factors. After World War II there was a general prosperity for the majority of Americans. Groups who continued to suffer from chronic unemployment came to be viewed as outsiders. In addition, such unemployment concentrated itself amongst minority groups because of pervasive job discrimination. Thus there was a higher proportion of minorities of color among the unemployed than represented in the population at large. The deviant status of the unemployed was intensified by racism. Many beliefs about the recipients of social services were simply restatements of the stereotypes about racial and cultural minorities.

The argument about the paucity of resources had some validity. Although the growth of the overall resources of the country more than covered the increase in the growth of social programs, two factors put a strain on available funds. First, a higher percentage of the budget was spent on the military, particularly after the onset of the Vietnam War. Second, the tax structure of the United States more and more shifted the burden of taxation away from corporations and the wealthy toward middle and working class Americans who represented the bulk of the voters. For these people the scarcity of resources manifested itself in increased taxation. They felt that an increasingly higher proportion of their income was being used to support, not the needy, but undeserving deviants and minorities.

Groups who were enjoying the advantages of the tax structure saw in tax revolt the opportunity to further increase their share of the nation's resources through an upward redistribution of income (Piven & Cloward, 1982, p. 7). In addition, unattractive social programs and high unemployment would give them greater control over the labor force by creating anxiety about layoffs among workers and a pool of unemployed who would gladly replace those holding jobs. Thus, pressures could be created to reduce wages and undermine labor unions (Ibid, p. 13). It has therefore been in their interest to support politicians and programs that have favored retrenchment. The resources of the wealthy have been used to popularize cutbacks through advertisement and other use of the mass media. In so doing they were no longer attacking programs that the middle and working class saw as relevant to their lives, but were supporting a preexisting distaste for unpopular expenditures.

Retrenchment and Social Work

As social programs became more unpopular, so did social workers. The relationship between social workers and social programs changed from the 1930s to the present. During the Roosevelt Administration social workers were among the chief architects of the Welfare State. However, many professionally trained workers began to disengage themselves from work with the poor. By the post World War II period almost all social workers with a Master of Social Work degree were not involved with this population in any meaningful way. Rather, they defined themselves as professional counselors (Cloward & Epstein, pp. 40–63).

During the early 1960s there was a rediscovery of poverty in America (Harrington). There was a renewed interest in programs that would address the problem, together with an expressed need for people with relevant expertise to administer these programs. In spite of their loss of interest in working with the poor, social workers with professional training were seen as needed experts. Undergraduate students were recruited into the profession by welfare departments through the use of grants and summer employment. State welfare training programs paid already employed welfare workers substantial grants to return to graduate school. In return for these grants the workers agreed to return to work at the welfare programs where they had been previously employed for a specified period of time, usually equivalent to the period that they went to school.

Many welfare workers took advantage of the opportunity for this education. Their training at graduate schools, however, was soon criticized as irrelevant to the task of working with the poor. Graduate programs were geared to teach psychotherapeutically oriented casework. Most of those trained through the grant programs left welfare work following their period of indenture for more lucrative and "challenging" work in the mental health and related areas. It was not long before the use of relatively well-paid "trained" social workers was seen as an unnecessary expense for welfare departments. The grants were gradually scrapped.

In the 1970s welfare programs separated "eligibility" from "services." The purpose of this was to eliminate the repetitive task of determining eligibility for professionally trained social workers. The more creative tasks related to psychotherapy would then be the sole tasks of the service workers. Less educated eligibility workers would tend to do the mundane tasks. Gradually the service jobs were decreased and service workers were encouraged to leave work in public assistance agencies. Eventually the programs became almost totally limited to the eligibility function.

While some social workers recognized that the separation might ultimately result in the removal of services from the public assistance programs, the separation was seen by others as a recognition of the professional nature of the social work task. The resource finding inherent in eligibility work was seen as repetitive and uncreative. The services function had more status. It was clinical in nature and required a creative expert who needed to separate himself or herself from the mundane so that there would be no interference with the complex tasks of professional functioning (Litwak, pp. 177–184). To the poor the expertise in resource finding and advocacy that might be available to them through a highly trained and skilled professional would have been considered a valuable resource. Instead, they were offered clinical services that seemed to many to be of questionable value. As the services function was deleted from public assistance programs there was little, if any, opposition from clients.

The surprising lack of interest and skill of social workers in the development of services for the poor and other disadvantaged groups have their roots in a long history of conflict in professional social work. This conflict, while dominated by one faction, has never been thoroughly resolved. The profession has indeed taken on the practice and ideological stance of the dominant group, a clinical anti-activist approach. However, it has always retained some identification and reputation as a profession involved in social action in spite of its lack of ability and recent lack of performance in this area. The paradox between the differences in the profession's functioning and reputation in social action are a result of its history, and a small remnant of activist practitioners that always remained in the profession. We will look at an overview of this history in terms of the jurisdictional disputes that took place, the dominant and subordinate groups during the conflicts, the nature of maintenance of control of the profession and the ways in which the profession's stance on social activism and reform was a reflection of the historical factionalism and the roles of each faction. This overview will provide a summary of the content that will be covered in detail in the chapters that follow.

Historical Overview

In the late nineteenth century idealists attempted to view society form a scientific perspective. Their hope was that a social science could be developed that would correct the evils of society just as effectively as physical science had improved the physical world for humankind. This group became the Social Science Movement and attracted members of agencies that addressed themselves to social problems such as charities, prison and health related issues and led to the formation of the American Social Science Association. They hoped that this association would provide theory that would be applicable to practice. The practitioners who hoped to apply this information eventually became members of the profession of social work.

The nature of social problems caused both the theorists and practitioners considerable difficulty. There were a variety of levels at which these problems could be attacked. One could attempt to change the structure of society to make the system more equitable. An alternative approach would be to work with the people suffering as a result of these problems and help them develop mechanisms to cope with the existing environment and make better use of available resources. Each of these positions had partisans in the newly developing profession of social work.

One group of social workers maintained their idealism. Their roots were in the feminist and abolitionist movements of the nineteenth century. They generally represented a well-to-do respected class whose relatively modest but sufficient resources were used to finance their ventures into social work. Their idea was that activism, voluntary sharing of material and intellectual resources, and contact and communication between different classes would result in understanding and mutual regard. This non-revolutionary process was supposed to gradually create a classless society and a true democracy. These social workers had initiated the process that resulted in the creation of Hull House and other similar establishments of the settlement movement.

The second group of social workers claimed to have many of the same ideological roots as the settlement people. However, their actions and priorities suggested different motives. Their base was an idealistic philosophy known as the "stewardship of wealth." Those who had acquired riches were seen as obliged to share their fortunes with the poor. They viewed themselves as divinely chosen stewards of wealth whose calling was to expand opportunity by creating jobs and by distributing the benefits of their God-given resources throughout the population. One of the means of doing this was through philanthropy, where funds were donated and then distributed to the needy.

In order to assure the efficient distribution of funds, agencies were created by the philanthropies to make determinations ensuring that money be given only to those truly in need. The agencies also sought to discourage ongoing dependency among the poor who could be rehabilitated to resume employment. The functionaries who administered the agencies and created programs that would accomplish these goals drew their leadership from a major philanthropic institution that came to be known as the Charity Organization Society.

These two groups, the settlement workers and the Charity Organization Society workers, developed different objectives and goals. Throughout the history of the profession, they have been in competition for the control of the direction of social work practice and education. This competition manifested itself in the jurisdictional disputes, the dominance of the profession, the maintenance of the control that became established, and the stance that social work eventually took regarding social activism. We will look at each of these manifestations and their eventual impact on social practice.

Jurisdictional Disputes

The major thrust of the initial battles between the Charity Organization Society workers and the settlement house workers centered around academic and educational issues. The Charity Organization people favored an approach that would speak to practice, i.e., provide information that would directly enhance the skills of practitioners.

They found concern with global theoretical knowledge a limited intellectual exercise with little value. The charity people pressed for a "practical stance" in the profession and in professional education.

The knowledge base of social work was the first area where this pressure was felt. The original social science orientation of the American Social Science Association was perceived as too cerebral and oriented toward theory. The resulting dispute caused the social workers to leave the social science parent organization and form an independent professional society called the National Conference of Charities and Corrections. Because of their leadership in the formation of the group, the charity organization practitioners dominated the new association.

Jurisdiction and control were also an issue when the professional schools were founded. Association with universities put academics in charge of professional education. The practitioners opposed such academic control of the programs for potential professionals on the grounds that such domination would lead to an emphasis on theory and insufficient attention to practical matters. The schools of social work were therefore set up as independent entities or with loose nominal affiliation to existing universities. In such institutions Charity Organization Society personnel had almost exclusive control of both administration and teaching.

As time passed, greater and greater pressure developed to incorporate these schools into bona fide institutions of higher learning. This pressure came largely from the settlement people who, together with other idealists, continued to favor a global theoretical approach and academic affiliation. Feeling the need for professional legitimization, the charity workers finally agreed to university affiliation. However, they were incorporated as separate graduate professional schools, where by minimizing contact with the academic community, practitioners were able to maintain a lion's share of control of all aspects of education programs.

The values and ideology of the Charity Organization Society were also reflected in the entry requirements for the schools and the profession, particularly the charity agencies. Early in the history of social work a picture of the ideal social worker was developed by the Charity Organization. This person possessed an assortment of personality traits. What was desired was a practical man who had achieved some success in life. He was to have good common sense, be fair, be of good moral character and have an aversion to politics. Intellectuals and academics were considered unsuitable because it was claimed that their education distracted them from the real world.

The settlement people, on the other hand, felt that education broadened a person and provided a resource to those whom he or she wished to serve. A person educated away from the real world would find social work an enlightening experience that would give true value to his efforts. It would be the medium whereby he could return to reality and make his theories meaningful through practical application.

The curriculum was also an arena for jurisdictional disputes. The Charity Organization Society's dominance of early social work education led to the criticism that schools of social work were the training facilities of that agency. They did not offer a broad education applicable to the diversity of interests that existed in the field at the time. Critics suggested that the profession would never be legitimized if it did not offer a more global education program. The debate led to agreement that social work education needed to be generic, i.e., applicable to all manner of social work practice rather than specific to one agency such as the Charity Organization Society.

The field searched for some years for a generic curriculum. This was the purpose of the Milford Conference in 1929. It presented the notion that a common element ran through all social work practice. This element was psychiatric theory, issues and terminology. An alliance with the profession of psychiatry was proposed to provide not only a claim to generativity, but an alliance that legitimated social work by associating it with a high status medical speciality.

In reality, beyond jargon and theoretical obfuscation, the psychiatric model supported existing Charity Organization Society practices. There was no need to make substantive changes. The Charity Organization Society was again able to assert its predominance in the field and its control over the direction of the profession.

Dominant Factions and the Practice, Education and Ideology of the Profession

Throughout the formative years of the profession from 1900 to 1930, the most influential faction was the Charity Organization Society. The settlement workers were not as effective in maintaining control. Their own practice involved social action and the education of clients, but they were limited in the effect they had on the profession. The character of the profession was established by the Charity Organization Society and caseworkers that shared their stance.

It was just after this institutionalization of social work practice and education that the Great Depression hit. The activities and policies of President Hoover mirrored the ideology of the Charity Organization Society about social services. This, in turn, was a reflection of the mainstream of pre-Depression America's belief about the subject. It was woefully inadequate in dealing with the results of the financial collapse.

What the Depression required was innovative social programs. Social work education in no way prepared its people to develop imaginative solutions to the unique problems of this era. The settlement workers, however, were much better prepared to face the demands of the Depression. Their work had given them the experience and skills to cope. This kind of creativity helped them create the social problems of the New Deal. President Roosevelt was a pragmatist open to new ideas. He allowed settlement social workers to become his closest advisers and to implement their ideas as part of his administration.

The status that resulted from such a close working relationship with the national administration brought a high degree of respect to the entire profession. The charity workers, recognizing this, yielded the leadership of the profession to the settlement workers for a time, and gave lip service to the goals of the New Deal. They maintained, however, their control in two key professional areas that kept them and their ideology alive as a viable force in social work. They retained their leadership positions in private non-governmental agencies and they continued to control professional education in the schools of social work.

The private agencies were totally unable to meet the relief needs of the Depression. This financial function was taken over by government. Social workers in the private agencies, relieved of their role in the distribution of financial assistance, dedicated themselves to the dominant method of practice in the field as they saw it: casework. Skills and techniques in casework became the substance of social work education and practice. The skills of the New Deal social workers never found their way into the curriculum. Their frequent appeals for public welfare content at the schools went unheeded. The profession continued to turn to a psychiatric-psychotherapeutic model for the justification of casework practice, legitimization and status.

This perspective viewed the client as a patient in need of a cure. Problems that he or she faced would be addressed through the modification and adjustment of intrapsychic functioning. The existence of environmental causes for problems, although accepted in theory, was minimized or ignored in practice.

The casework orientation had its impact upon students too. To be a psychotherapist one needed to be well adjusted. The students faced a quasi-psychotherapeutic learning experience. Students were subjected to judgmental and arbitrary standards that often enforced conformity rather than encouraged academic or practice performance.

Two additional factions developed during the Depression years. The functionalists fully supported the major casework concepts but took an even more conservative view than the Charity Organization Society. Drawing their theory from Rankian Psychology, they totally rejected active participation of the caseworker in the client's life including any kind of advocacy or social action on his or her behalf. The caseworker's role was only to provide the relationship that would enable the client to develop insight, express himself or herself, and thereby be able to adjust internal psychological mechanisms. This, in turn, was supposed to make it possible for the client to solve his or her environmental or interpersonal problems. Any personal intervention by the therapist was seen as robbing the client of his or her freedom of choice. In spite of a strong theoretical commitment to freedom of choice, the teachers and therapists of the functional school played an extremely domineering role with clients and students.

Exactly the opposite position was taken by another faction which developed during the 1930s. This was a left-wing movement called the "Rank and File." Although they did not fully reject casework as a method of practice, they strongly supported aggressive social action and environmental involvement. In general, they supported the New Deal programs but were quick to call the liberals to task when there was any indication of reneging on the promise of assistance to the poor. They represented a diversity of left-wing opinion. Although they saw some progress in Welfare State politics they felt that ultimately there was a need for the restructuring of American society and a true and equitable redistribution of wealth (Spano, p. 2).

The Rank and File movement was destroyed during the red scare of the McCarthy era. Their union was expelled from the C.I.O. for so called "communist domination." Thereafter, anyone associated with the union could not find an agency job. The profession, in general, disavowed its relationship with the Rank and File and disregarded the injustices done to them. The ideas of the group were submerged and not heard again until the late 1960s.

The functionalists had more impact on the field than the Rank and Filers. While their esoteric adherence to Rankian psychology was generally rejected, their passive therapeutic method emphasizing intrapsychic phenomena became the general method of casework practice. Also to become part of the mainstream was emphasis on the personality of the therapist, the interpretation of the concept of resistance and the punitive and domineering stance of the teacher and therapist toward students and clients.

It was this kind of posture that came to characterize casework and social work education during the post World War II period. When the need for creativity and leadership again arose during the 1960s, these casework-therapy-oriented social workers were ill prepared for the task. Some critics saw incompetence and the denigration of clients inherent in the casework philosophy. This alienated the poor. The later decline in public opinion of liberal welfare state programs further deprived the profession of a supporting constituency. This has led to a general decline in the status of social work and social service programs.

Social work retains its casework methodology and ideology. As in the 1950s, the profession has increasingly eschewed the involvement in social action that characterized the 1960s and early 1970s. Practice as psychotherapy, it is apparently felt, will be the safest haven in these difficult times.

Activism, Reform and the History of Social Work Education and Practice

The point of greatest division in the field of social work has been the issue of social reform. The original purpose of the social science idealists was to create a science and practice that would alter society in the interest of equity and put an end to such social problems as poverty. That position was not supported by the philanthropists who supported casework agencies. Social reform obviously would upset the structure that gave the philanthropists their position of privilege. Psychodynamically oriented casework, a curriculum stressing individual problems and the glorification of an atheoretical, non-intellectual, apolitical profession served to take social work out of the social reform arena.

The settlement people spent some of their efforts in reform activities. Although some of their ideas bore fruit, the profession never took up the thrust of their activities as part of its tradition. As the success and importance of the reformers diminished there was no one to continue their task. Past victories have become hollow as, gradually, the programs that have been said to have remade American society, have been and are being dismantled. At this point in history a reconstruction of social service may have to come from a quarter other than social work since a large proportion of the profession seem to again be seeking refuge in noncontroversial activities, hoping to save their professional lives from the wrath of conservatives.

When engaged in reform activities social workers have chosen a liberal rather than a socialist foundation. Liberals believe that the generation of voter support and the implementation and creation of laws will ensure continuation and enforcement within the existing governmental system. From this perspective social work cannot be apolitical. It must always maintain some activism in order to survive.

According to the socialist stance, true social reform is not possible within the existing system since it is controlled by capitalist interests. Reformers, if they are to be truly successful, must aim toward putting an end to capitalism and replace it with a political system that serves the people. The mainstream of social work practice never accepted socialism. The Charity Organization Society viewed it with horror, suggesting that reform would draw the profession into socialist ideology.

The settlement people were committed to social reform in the interest of the preservation of capitalism. They felt that there was a common interest between classes created by a need to preserve the system. This common interest would lead the wealthy to share their resources to forestall the discontent that might lead to revolution. The settlement workers saw themselves as experts who would identify the needs to which resources could be applied, enhance communication between classes and act as a conduit for good feeling and cooperation that would ultimately result in a classless society without revolution.

Even the socialists amongst the settlement people chose the non-revolutionary avenue for their reform efforts. With the exception of members of the Rank and File movement of the Depression, the notion of restructuring society for so-called "genuine" reform was not raised again until the 1960s and 1970s by a small group of radicals in the profession.

Implications

As we shall show, there is little question that successful reform within a non-revolutionary context in a Capitalist society remains a possibility. It is within this context that the field of social work has and can continue to play a substantive role. Within that role the profession has prospered and had its proudest moments.

Social workers who only function outside a reform perspective serve not their clients but the very people who would destroy the profession and all that it represents. In the early years of social work an association between philanthropists and practitioners committed to "do good" sweetened the sour image of the "robber baron". Today the privileged do not need social work programs to create a positive image. Advertisement and mass media can be used to influence and control public opinion. Those who wish to rid themselves of the financial burden of social services can use the media to discredit the profession and its programs. Often they remain unchallenged in their negative portrayal of human services because of apathy or the great expense of rebuttal.

The strategy of laying low by restricting practice to apolitical psychotherapy also has other limitations. The ideology of casework is shared by many groups. As such, those who develop and implement policies based upon it need not be social workers. Herbert Hoover was a good example of a non-social worker who functioned without social work advisers. His programs and ideas were identical to those of the Charity Organization Society. They failed because they did not adequately address the problems of the day. What was required at the time was innovation and the experts to develop it. Social workers, in developing creative solutions during the New Deal reform period, acted as such advisers to the Administration. Trained social work innovators would again bring to society the expertise that is unique to their profession.

When social work functions in a wide variety of spheres it is a unique profession. The practice of psychotherapy is the province of a wide group of practitioners. It is practiced today by psychiatrists, psychologists, counselors, school personnel and myriads of others. As programs are cut and jobs become more scarce, social workers will find themselves more and more in competition with these groups for positions. In addition, serious questions are still being raised whether psychotherapy is in any way effective. Thus, both in terms of competition and accomplishment, a social work profession limited exclusively to this area of practice is in a dubious position.

As a reform profession during the 1930s social work served a satisfied constituency. Never before or since has the profession enjoyed such respectability and status. Furthermore, its clientele and the people it served were the same. As it faces an uncertain future, the profession can gain strength by fulfilling its original commitment for social change in the interest of solving social problems. Although such a strategy seems risky at first glance, the lesson of the history we present in *Philanthropists, Therapists and Activists* suggests that it is a way to preserve not only the profession's performance but also its usefulness and integrity.

Chapter 2
The Professionalization of Charity

Charity, the generous act of sharing resources with the poor or organizations that tend their needs or the needs of other unfortunates, is a cornerstone of all religious doctrine. This sharing of wealth is looked upon as a sacred duty. Yet, in different religions and cultures the concept is interpreted differently. American Protestantism with roots in Puritanism had particular difficulty; while the religion held to a standard requirement of charity, it also was rooted in a concept known as the "work ethic." Elements of the two ideas conflicted and needed to be reconciled.

Like charity, work was a sacred duty. Those who were lazy and shiftless were considered sinful and unworthy of assistance. The misery of poverty was their just desserts and was seen as eventually making them so uncomfortable that they would be motivated to mend their ways. Charity given to the unworthy was not only wasted, but served to forestall their rehabilitation by alleviating the pain that was the natural consequence of their indolence. Hence, they would not be motivated to change.

Yet, in the eyes of the Puritans there was another class of poor. Their poverty was seen as not of their own making and not subject to amelioration through a change in their behavior. These were the "worthy" poor, and consisted of widows, orphans, the aged, infirm, crippled and insane. Their care was an obligation defined by Christian charity.

In practice the difference between the worthy and unworthy poor was not always easy to determine. This delineation, together with the administration of assistance and the maintenance of institutions for the poor, eventually became the province of a group of people who considered themselves as having special skills and expertise. They were known first as overseers of the poor and then as charity workers. Together with those who operated prisons, they gradually formed part of what was to become social work. In effect it was their role to resolve the conflict between charity and the work ethic.

The Conflict of Charity and the Work Ethic in American Philanthropic Ideology

Although charity remained in the domain of church functions, in England it gradually also came under the jurisdiction of secular government. Under Queen Elizabeth I the rules under which those in authority would assist the poor became codified. These reflected the needs and beliefs of those who controlled the budding industrialization of England as well as the religious notions of the time. Relief needed to make the recipient uncomfortable enough so that he or she would be willing to take a low-paying job instead of charity. Thus the work ethic of the churches supported secular industrial needs and was an integral part of what would come to be called "poor law." In 1601 the Elizabethan Poor Law came into being in England and provided a legal framework for work relief and indenture of the poor.

Like the English, the Americans made provisions for the care of the poor in their early governments. Yet, also like the English, they placed limitations on the administration of charity. They, too, demanded that the able-bodied poor work for what they received. Indeed the Puritan work ethic was even more emphatic than the Elizabethan Poor Law (Bendix, pp. 61–62). This Puritan philosophy dominated New England during the colonial period.

The encouragement of idleness was seen as the end result of improperly administered charity, i.e., assisting the able bodied. A person who received such assistance was in danger of losing his or her self-respect and falling into an ongoing condition of dependency and continued laziness called "pauperism." To prevent this disease-like pauperation, overseers of the poor came to control the administration of charity.

The conflict between Christian charity and the belief that charity, in effect, encouraged sinfulness made it most difficult to raise funds even for the most praiseworthy of projects. It did indeed require the skill of an expert to present programs needing philanthropic support in such a way that they appeared to support the welfare of the general community as well as the poor. In addition, the giver needed to be guaranteed that the gift would be used in a worthy cause and not encourage sin. No less a talent than Benjamin Franklin was engaged by a physician to help raise money for the first hospital in America in 1751. Using his skill at diplomacy and planning, Franklin was able to develop a funding program with a board of directors that assured the reluctant contributors that there would be no abuse of the project. In addition, he introduced a complex plan of voluntary contributions and matching government funds. This assured the contributors a reputation for generosity beyond their investment, and also their getting more than their money's worth (Franklin, pp. 6–7).

Franklin's appeals for contributions made liberal use of the concept that the rich had an obligation to those who were not as fortunate as they were. His pleas included many references to the rewards and gratification of acting in a humane way.

Can any thing in this checkered world, afford more real and lasting satisfaction to humane minds, than the reflection of having made such a social use of the favor of Providence, as renders them, in some measure, instruments which open the door of ease and comfort to such as are bowed down with poverty and sickness; and which may be a means of increasing the number of people, and preserving many useful members to the public from ruin and distress (Pumphery & Pumphery, p. 42).

Franklin's skill made his approach a prototype for American charitable appeals thereafter. The money contributed would be stretched by matching funds. Involvement in the program itself by philanthropists would assure the appropriate use of the charity. Finally, the self-interest of the contributor would be served through the enhancement of his or her reputation, the fulfillment of religious and ethical obligations and the pleasure of being engaged in the inherently worthwhile endeavor of doing good. Philanthropy justified in this way, became a part of the life of American businessmen.

The Proliferation of Charitable Organizations

The personal appeal to the benevolent instincts of the philanthropists was specific to a particular need that appealed to the fund raiser. In each case the argument used included references to how efficiently the monies would be used and serve only the deserving. Philanthropists had to make judgments about their contributions. Many felt the need to educate themselves to make the proper decisions and sometimes to become even more deeply involved in the administration of the program by being board members or even directors of the agencies.

Because of the degree of personal involvement, each philanthropist gave to charities that reflected his or her own interests and biases. Elias Boudinot, the first president of the American Bible Society bequeathed a substantial amount for the purchase of eyeglasses for the aged poor. John Jacob Astor made one of his rare contributions to the

Association for the Relief of Respectable Aged and Indigent Females. Other benefactors founded groups that reflected interests such as temperance, abolition, moral reform, the formation of an American Negro state in Africa, the foundation and support of various colleges and universities, monument construction, children's aid, prevention of pauperism, hospital construction and improvement, prevention of and assistance of victims of various infirmities, and prison reform. The feeling that it was the prerogative of the giver to decide how his generosity would be used was summed up by William Appleton: "I part with money in various ways of charity but much like to do it in my own way and not to be dictated to or even asked but in a general way, to give with others" (Bremner, p. 46).

To critics, this attitude reflected more the fancy of the giver rather than the needs of the benefactor. For this reason the criticism was spawned that philanthropy was self-serving. Ralph Waldo Emerson wrote:

> If malice and vanity wear the coat of philanthropy, shall that pass? . . . I tell thee thou foolish philanthropist, that I grudge the dollar, the dime, the cent I give to such men as do not belong to me and to whom I do not belong. There is a class of persons to whom by all spiritual affinity I am bought and sold; for them I would go to prison if need be; but your miscellaneous popular charities; the education at college of fools; the building of meeting-houses to the vain end to which many now stand; alms to sots, and the thousandfold Relief Societies;—though I confess with shame I sometimes succumb and give the dollar, it is a wicked dollar, which by and by I shall have the manhood to withhold (Emerson, p. 3).

Whether the motive was guilt, hypocrisy, or vanity, the development of charitable organizations based upon the interests of wealthy individuals created a plethora of agencies designed to deal with very specific kinds of problems. In some cases there were abundant funds to deal with trivial problems or problems that affected a very few people. In other cases widespread and serious problems languished for lack of money. The randomness of this philanthropy was also said to foster duplication of services and assistance without rhyme or reason.

By the late 1800s, the wastefulness of uncoordinated charities became the subject of a moral crusade. The proliferation had created a "Benevolent Empire." Philanthropy needed to be made into a science that codified the administration of philanthropic programs. The need to cope with the morass of agencies together with the need to examine clientele for merit and the proper amount of assistance required professional experts. Out of the need for experts there developed a coordinating agency called the Charity Organization Society. The group developed a dynamic leader, Mary Richmond, who led the movement in the direction of professionalization of charity work.

Jane Addams, another charismatic social work leader, led another group of social work agencies, the settlement houses. Although many of the goals and roots of this movement were different than those of the charity workers, both groups considered themselves and each other members of the same profession. Both also were active in different ways during the Progressive Era when they worked to professionalize the field. Their interaction and conflicts during this time form the foundation of the struggles that were to repeat themselves through the history of social work.

Mary Richmond and the Charity Organization Society

The Charity Organization Society first appeared in England in 1869. It was quickly transported to the United States by the Rev. Stephen Gurteen of Buffalo, New York, who organized the society in 1877. The purpose of the organization was to practice "scientific philanthropy." This was the notion that a systematic approach to the distribution of charity would prevent pauperism, the distribution of funds to the undeserving able-bodied poor and the duplication of grants to individuals by more than one agency. The idea spread, and by 1879 more than a dozen cities had organized their own Charity Organization Societies. In 1891 Mary Richmond became the director of the Baltimore Charity Organization Society and thereafter became the major spokesperson for that organization as well as the most important leader in social work's professional organizations (Leiby, pp. 111–120).

Unlike many of her contemporary colleagues in social work Richmond was not born into a wealthy family. Rather, her parents passed away soon after her birth in 1861. She was raised by relatives who were not well off. In 1878 she graduated from high school and went to New York City to work as a clerical worker. There she apparently continued to educate herself and attended lectures at Cooper Union, a progressive institution of higher education. She was hired as a clerk by the Baltimore Charity Organization Society in 1889 but in only two years she had risen through the ranks to become the director of that agency (Colcord & Mann, pp. 15–18, 31).

The Charity Organization at first described its role as the investigation of applications for assistance, sorting out the deserving from the undeserving poor for cooperating agencies. In addition, a register of recipients was prepared for all agencies to prevent the duplication of assistance. Rev. Gurteen's statement in 1877 illustrates the point.

> The basic axiom, the cardinal principle of the 'Charity Organization Society' is diametrically opposed to all systems, all institutions, all charities, all forms of relief whatsoever, which avowedly or tacitly adopt the creed of Charles Lamb to 'give and ask no questions,' or which is worse, that system of injudicious questioning at the door, or on the street, which leads the beggar to invent additional falsehoods. The fundamental law of its operation is expressed in one word, 'INVESTI-GATE.' Its motto is: 'No relief (except in the extreme cases of despair or imminent death) without previous and searching examination . . . . This work-test is one of the most perfect touchstones for discriminating between the deserving and undeserving that has ever been devised . . . . (Pumphery & Pumphery, pp. 170–171).

This Charity Organization Society was to become the consultant agency providing the expertise for "scientific philanthropy." The so-called "Social Sciences" were to be applied to this field. Major universities had included them in their curriculum as legitimate areas of study. The application of these sciences by experts in human behavior could be helpful in the appropriate distribution of charity. While the Charity Organization Society had no relief resources of its own, it made this expertise available to agencies that did.

The role of investigation was part of the detection of fraud, what Gurteen called its "repressive work." The Charity Organization Society, in making financial resources available, did its "benevolent work." Beyond these two functions there were two other areas of service that were seen as appropriate for the agency providing "scientific charity": "provident work" and "reformatory work" (Pumphery & Pumphery, p. 172).

Provident work and reformatory work go beyond the actual giving of assistance, the detection of fraud or eligibility related to assistance. Rather, they involve the application of certain interpersonal skills, supposedly a dimension of the expertise of agency personnel, for the benefit of the client. Provident work was aimed at helping the client to change his or her behavior and personality so that the weaknesses that promoted poverty and pauperism could be minimized or eliminated. The medium for this change was the relationship between the client and a member of the agency staff.

Reformatory work sought to strike out at forces that took advantage of the poor, kept them in their state of poverty and oppressed and otherwise treated them unfairly. The agency was to use its office's political power and the ability of its staff to organize groups of people to fight and otherwise oppose these conditions. Examples of areas to be addressed by reformatory work included correcting poor housing, preventing unhealthy sanitation, discouraging business practices that appeared to be directed specifically toward the poor, promoting the temperance movement and dealing with other social abuses.

The two elements of provident and benevolent work were said to present the agency with an unmanagable task. Eventually the focus of the agency shifted in the direction of concentrating upon provident work which was to become friendly visiting and finally to what is now casework. This shift was claimed to be done in the interest of efficient use of time.

By the time Mary Richmond became the head of the Baltimore Charity Organization Society in 1891 the scope of practice had already been narrowed to concern with individual clients' problems. It was her justification of this role definition that institutionalized it and presented it as a logical choice in the interest of better service. To be effective one had to circumscribe his or her efforts to manageable specifics. This, too, was reform and involved making changes in a specific client's life space. It included assistance such as enrolling a child in a special education program, moving a family out of unsanitary conditions, or appealing to a landlord or other entrepreneur to extend credit to a specific client. Richmond called this kind of reform the "retail method" of reform. She referred to agitation for general societal change as the "wholesale method" of reform (Colcord & Mann, pp. 214–247).

Mary Richmond's major concern was the codification and development of the method by which one could be effective at friendly visiting casework. Her work in this area related to two dimensions: the initial sorting out of all of the many facets of a client's problem as perceived by a skilled practitioner—called "diagnosis"—and the method for the implementation of a plan for the amelioration of these difficulties.

The basis for the concept of diagnosis can be found in the investigatory procedures involved in the careful scrutiny of each client's application for assistance to determine the specifics of his or her needs, the existing resources for the client to draw upon, the appropriate assistance to render (satisfying the need without fostering dependency), and the particular agency equipped to deal with the need so that a good referral could be made. Although much was made of the point that such investigation was in the client's best interest, i.e., preventing dependency, it is also apparent that a major goal of the investigation was the prevention of fraud and the minimal use of funds.

The preoccupation with diagnosis and investigation, taken together with the notion of "retail reform," led the Charity Organization Society out of the arena of politically oriented reform. The settlement social workers, another group, were not so adverse to political involvement and "wholesale reform." They actively engaged in more global efforts for social change.

Jane Addams and the Settlement Movement

In England and America settlement houses grew out of movements dominated by socially-minded clergy. They sought, for a variety of reasons—some paternalistic, some missionary, and some even Marxist—to live in communities where poor people lived and to share the skills and knowledge they gained from their education. The first English settlement, Toynbee Hall, opened in 1884 and was directed by an Episcopalian priest, Rev. Samuel Barnett. Supported by the students and professors of Oxford University, the idea flourished and took hold. However, it did not become the significant institution that it was to become in the United States.

America had begun to experience wave upon wave of immigration as it progressed through the industrial revolution. The resulting poverty and upheaval created the ideal medium for the growth of the settlement movement. The American experience differed from the English experience in two significant ways. First, the clergy was responding to the failure of earlier Protestant mission efforts, such as the Salvation Army, to spread good will. The blatant mixture of salvation and charity not only had failed to gain popularity among the new immigrants, but also did not sit well with the ideal of good work for its own sake held by many of the involved liberal clergymen (Leiby, p. 128).

A second important difference between the American and English settlement movements was the involvement of women in the United States. Many American reformers left the abolition movement after the ratification of the thirteenth amendment and turned to other liberal causes such as women's suffrage. Among them were not only men such as William Lloyd Garrison and Wendall Phillips, but also many dynamic and active women (Schlessinger, 1951, pp. 107, 113–116). A substantial number of these women had been educated in the new college programs that had recently become available to them. Most traditional professions were closed to women. The settlement movement and social work in general became an opportunity for them to become engaged in useful endeavors by putting their newly learned skills to use (Lunt, pp. 93–106).

Stanton Coit founded the first American settlement house in New York in 1886, at first called Neighborhood Guild, and then University Settlement. In 1887 Vida Scudder, having just returned from a visit to Oxford, met with other recent graduates from Smith, Vassar, Wellesley, Bryn Mawr and Radcliffe and proposed a "college settlement for women." The College Settlements Association was founded out of this group in 1889. In 1892 this Association founded settlements in New York, Boston and Philadelphia. In addition, two members, Jane Addams and Ellen Starr, founded in Chicago what was to become the most famous of the settlement houses, Hull House. Following this development, Graham Taylor, a professor at Chicago Theological Seminary, established Chicago Commons in 1894 for the advancement of what he called "Christian sociology."

Although the movement mushroomed from these beginnings, by far the most well-known and influential leader of the settlement movement was Jane Addams of Hull House. Her ideas and those she influenced were as important as Mary Richmond's in the developing foundation of the new profession of social work.

Jane Addams was born in 1860 in the rural Illinois town of Cedarville to a Quaker and upper middle-class family. Her father was involved in politics and that subject was frequently a part of family discussions. Jane Addams' mother died when she was a child and her father remarried into a prominent family. Jane's early education was at Rockford Seminary, a school with a strong missionary tradition. The ideal of raising children in the country, pacifism, her father's reform politics and honesty, and her Christian education are recurrent themes in her work and writings. The enormous impact of Jane Addams and the settlements is described by Morrison and Commager:

> The influence of the social settlements was felt in time not only in the slums but in the legislative chambers, in labor reforms, in health and sanitation, in arts and handicrafts. Social workers, regarded by politicians and businessmen as misguided zealots, came to be recognized as the most effective reformers of their generation. Certainly that was true of Jane Addams, who founded Hull House. . . . Hull House became in time a world institution, and Jane Addams more nearly a world figure than any other woman of her day (p. 458).

Three factors were identified as motivating workers who had become involved in the settlement movement (Addams, 1910, pp. 113–127). The first was social democracy in a classless, quasi-capitalist state. The second had to do with the sharing of the "race life." This involved bringing education and culture to lower class groups who had been deprived of the opportunity to share these cultural resources. Finally, Addams speaks of a return to earlier Christian ideals of a community of people of equal status without regard to wealth. The absence of paternalism was to emulate the true democracy of the early church.

To start a settlement, young idealistic people with financial resources rented houses in communities where people were poor. The house was then occupied by the renters and opened to neighbors. After overcoming varying degrees of their potential client's initial hesitancy to become involved, the residents began developing relationships with their neighbors. They then were able to initiate a cultural program. Hull House's program began when Italian neighbors were invited to share slides of Italian art and listen to George Eliot's *Romola* read in Italian.

The settlements developed additional roles as they became institutionalized in Chicago and other cities. At first it was thought that the settlement could be a laboratory and experimental station for the new science of sociology. However, the nature of sociological research expanded rapidly, and subject areas of interest to sociologists quickly became far broader than could be examined in these settlements. This research component was nonetheless retained as a component of another role undertaken by the settlement workers: social reform. Data and empirical studies played an important part in reports that were to become a major part of the push to improve conditions for poor Americans.

In the areas of health, housing, child welfare, schools, recreation, welfare, working conditions and child labor, to name just a few, the settlements became the leading edge of a growing reform movement. Even in the area of civil rights for black Americans, a turn-of-the-century cause taboo for all but the most courageous of reformers, settlement workers played a leadership role. Their efforts helped in the formation of organizations such as the N.A.A.C.P.

The politicization of the movement led to many members, including Jane Addams (who delivered a nominating speech for Theodore Roosevelt at the Bull Moose Party Convention), becoming part of the Progressive Movement. In addition, a few well-known settlement workers such as Vida Scudder and Florence Kelly played an active role in the socialist movement. Other socialist workers such as Phillip Davis and Robert Hunter left the settlement movement claiming that their involvement kept their radicalism in check (Davis, p. 242).

Club work was the third role played by the settlements. The effort was to have the agency provide recreation and educational opportunity for children and others from slums. Particular emphasis was placed on the idea that the settlement was part of the community it served. People interested in participating came to the agency for its services rather than having a worker go to them. Settlement workers spoke of the three Rs of their movement: "Residence, Research, and Reform" (Trattner, p. 140).

The Settlement Movement and the Charity Organization Societies had come to maturity during the first twenty years of this century. This was a time of political change known as the Progressive Era. The issues of importance in that era included business reform, immigration and social reform. Social work was intimately involved in grappling with these issues. The various controversies and attempted resolutions of these controversies became a permanent part of the social work scene because the field became a profession at that time.

The Progressive Era

Industrialization, the sense of *noblesse oblige,* the existence of labor unrest and the threat of the development of a politically viable socialist movement at the turn of the century gave rise to a coalition of businessmen, intellectuals, and moral and religious leaders. This coalition viewed its goal as the improvement of the human condition and the control of corruption within the capitalist structure. It was known as the Progressive Movement.

Business was seen in need of reform in two ways. First, it needed to be controlled and prevented from throwing all caution to the wind in its pursuit of profit and power and endangering the democratic political process and the public's interest. Second, business needed to be encouraged to assume the responsibility of curing society's ills by sharing some of its resources. "Enlightened" businessmen became part of the core of the leadership of this movement in alliance with moral and spiritual leaders, including social workers.

Reform and American Business. The rapid industrialization and expansion of the United States during the nineteenth century led to excesses and unfair practices of American business in the opinion of reformers. The Progressive reformers characterized themselves as pledged to the regulation of business practices and the provision of social services. What is most noteworthy about the movement is that the backbone of its support and leadership came partially from the business community itself. These businessmen appeared to be an integral part of the movement committed to the regulation of business.

This peculiar state of affairs has been the subject of much investigation and controversy. Hofstadter identifies two classes of the wealthy:

old wealth, known as "mugwumps," and new wealth, those who had more recently acquired riches as a result of the industrial-technological revolution (1955, pp. 131–46). The mugwumps resented these pre-tenders to status. Those with old wealth looked with disdain upon these *nouveaux riches* and set themselves apart from them. They saw themselves as a kind of aristocracy; responsible and fair, having ac-quired their wealth through reputable means and feeling a sense of concern for all levels of society, particularly those who had been vic-timized by the rapid expansion of American industry:

> The industrialists were held to be uneducated and uncultivated, irre-sponsible, rootless and corrupt, devoid of refinement or or any sense of noblesse. "If our civilization is destroyed, as Macaulay predicted," wrote Henry Dedmares Lloyd in assessment of the robber barons, "it will not be by his barbarians from below. Our barbarians come from above.

> Our great money-makers have sprung in one generation into seats of power kings do not know. *The forces and the wealth are new, and have been the opportunity of new men. Without restraints of culture, experi-ence, the pride, or even the inherited caution of class or rank,* these men, intoxicated, think they are the wave instead of the float, and that they have created the business which has created them. To them science is but a never ending repertoire of investments stored up by nature for the syndicates, government but a fountain of franchises, the nations but customers in squads, and a million the unit of a new arithmetic of wealth written for them. They claim a power without control, exercised through forms which make it secret, anonymous, and perpetual. The possibilities of its gratification have been widening before them without interruption since they began, and even at a thousand millions they will feel no satisfaction and will see no place to stop" (Ibid., p. 141).

Morrison and Commager view the Progressives as tackling, with some success, the problems that America faced at that time. These involved the moral crisis brought on by a movement away from an agrarian society, the rise of big business, unequal distribution of wealth, the rise of the city and bossism (1962, p. 443). They suggest that, "the new social sins were impersonal and without evil intent . . ." (Ibid., p. 445) and led the more thoughtful of businessmen to become part of the reform movement that ultimately brought the changes the reestablished democratic stability. The evils of the corporation were attacked by the "trust busting" activities of Theodore Roosevelt, the "New Freedom" of Wilson and the reform effort of LaFollett. The program of the discrepancies in the distribution of wealth,

—though it seemed formidabe, proved in the end to be the easiest [problem] to solve. The solution was twofold. First the income tax— permitted by the Sixteenth Amendment and enacted in 1913—which made possible the orderly control of great fortunes. The second was a development unplanned and unforeseen which came only after the Second World War—the general leveling up of incomes so that the great majority of Americans could enjoy the benefits of an affluent society (Ibid., pp. 448–449).

During the current era of retrenchment the above statement seems incredible, particularly in that it comes from a history text that was standard in colleges and universities in the 1950s and 1960s. The literature abounds with material dealing with abuses of income tax law as well as the enduring American problem of poverty and the unequal distribution of wealth. There are many critiques of the Progressive Movement's leadership and the discrepancy between its stated goals and the actual outcome of its efforts. The difficulties are seen as an artifact of the political position taken by the reformers (Hofstadter, 1955, pp. 18–22).

The Progressives characterized themselves as attempting to minimize the dangers from the right and left. They were concerned with the exploitation of labor and the conditions of the masses. However, they openly and with few exceptions eschewed radicalism and socialism. It was the role of the reformer, as they saw it, to improve conditions within the capitalist structure. They set out to reform business, restore and maintain competition, and regulate monopoly. They were concerned with social issues including poverty, relations between capital and labor, slum conditions, and child and female labor. They represented a stance of communality and cooperation rather than struggle and confrontation. Most importantly they were intensely committed to the notion of private property.

The ethical framework of the movement carried it beyond the notion of *noblesse oblige*. The Progressives were tied to the "social gospel," a mixture of Christianity and a "socialism of the heart," seeking to create change through the implementation of law rather than through the revolutionary restructuring of society. The wealthy, by sharing some of their wealth and seeing to the needs of all, assured the longevity of capitalism by providing the poor and working classes an alternative to socialism and anarchy. Even the relationship between labor and management need not be one of confrontation, according to this view. Did not both benefit from production? Surely a more cooperative relationship, a syndicate, between labor and a corporation functioning in the role of a benevolent feudal lord would benefit all concerned.

Progressive reform, in many respects, was not reform at all to some historians, but rather a means by which business, under the guise of promoting social justice, could develop political control over government. By advocating reforms:

> . . . businessmen were able to harness to their own ends the desire of intellectuals and middle class reformers to bring together the thoughtful men of all classes in a 'vanguard for the building of a good community' (Weinstein, p. ix).

Weinstein's opinion is that the reformer played into the hands of the capitalists by coopting the "liberals" among them into the Progressive movement. This cooptation served to maintain the existing order and to prevent the threat of a working class revolution.

> But even for [those progressives who understood the role they were playing] the promotion of reform was not an act of cynicism: they simply sought a way to be immediately effective, to have real influence. Their purpose was not only to serve as defenders of the social system, but also to improve the human condition. In the most profound sense they failed, and badly; yet they were a good deal more than simply lackeys of the capitalist class (Ibid, p. xi).

The threat of the growth of socialism and the attack against business were very real in the late nineteenth century and the early part of the twentieth century. Labor had begun to assert itself with the formation of the Noble Order of the Knights of Labor in 1869. A more establishment-oriented representative of labor, the A.F. of L. was founded in 1886. In 1905 the Industrial Workers of the World (I.W.W. of Wobblies) came into existence and began taking hold. It was unabashedly revolutionary and committed to a socialist perspective.

With the growth of the labor movement, strikes, violence and unrest grew out of confrontation. Among the most famous of these were the Haymarket Riot of 1886, the Homestead Strike of 1892 and the Pullman Strike of 1894 under the leadership of Eugene V. Debs.

Debs was not only a dramatic and magnetic labor leader but the most successful American Socialist presidential candidate in history. In 1904 he polled 408,000 votes, four times the socialist vote of 1900. In 1908 Debs received 420,000 votes and in 1912 over 900,000 votes. In 1910 the Socialists elected their first congressman, Victor Berger, and the mayor of Milwaukee. In 1911 they elected mayors in 73 municipalities and 1200 lesser officials in 340 cities and towns.

From a capitalist perspective a genuine threat existed to their system at the time the Progressive coalition began to take shape. This coalition presented itself as the humanitarian alternative to this growing socialist movement. Through its programs capitalism could be prevented from victimizing the public and even become a vehicle for the just sharing of resources. All this could be accomplished without changing the basic economic structure of society by revolution.

The fact remains that, however grandiose and well meaning most reform programs seemed when planned and presented, they are often seen as almost always failing to achieve their goals (Hofstadter, 1955, p. 252). This applies not only to business reform proposals but also to philanthropic programs where the seeds of failure were planted into the very program structure (Galper, p. 5). What occurred was the appearance of benevolent intent whose goals could not be achieved because of some defect in the implementation or structure of the program. Thus the failure seemed to serve the purpose of creating the illusion of humanitarianism without the cost of viable programs and may be viewed as a deliberate dimension of the program plan.

The reformers and social workers of the Progressive Era did not see failure as an integral part of their programs. It was to them a characteristic of the breaking of new ground, a leakage in the mechanics in the delivery of the rewards of their proposals. What was required was a new knowledge base that would identify the reasons for failure and a group of expert professionals that could apply this knowledge in a "scientific" way that would create success. Social work saw itself as having the potential of developing into just such a profession. What it lacked was legitimization and consistent expertise among practitioners. The proponent of this view sought to make social work into a *bona fide* profession. They based their position upon the notion that their skills offered the poor benefits that were otherwise unavailable to them. They could be helpful beyond charity.

Many people involved in reform at that time, particularly those who came from the labor movement, were not so positive in their view. To them social workers who were involved in charity work were parties to hypocrisy. Rather than helping the poor, their activities were viewed by them as repressive.

The settlement movement also had its critics. Most came from those who differed from them politically. However, the settlement people themselves had the ability to look at their work critically and attempt to deal with their own shortcomings.

The most important controversy came from the interaction between Charities and Settlements. Because of their different ideologies they vied with each other to dominate the field in terms of determining its future direction. As they criticized each other there emerged the major controversies that repeat themselves through the history of the profession.

Social work professionalism was seen in quite a different light by social reformers of the developing labor movement. To them this movement offered a sop to quiet those who were reacting against the oppression of capitalism and hindered the organizational efforts of those committed to change.

Many suggested that charity would be unnecessary if workers were paid a fair wage (Crafts, pp. 19–24). Thus charity is "conscience money" for poor wages. Business can, it was argued, reduce or eliminate dividends rather than force working people to accept charity in hard times. The Charity Organization Society was looked upon as an agent of greedy capitalists:

> Such societies or churches are often little scrupulous concerning the sources from which their money is derived. They are too often willing to act as the alms giver of those who have amassed enormous fortunes for themselves in some licensed or unlicensed form of preying upon their fellow mortals. In so doing these churches or societies come to the support of a damaged reputation, which seeks to retrieve itself by a lavish display of benevolence after the fact, and justly expose themselves to the suspicion of condoning the original offense. Sometimes the largest givers are employers of labor who have persistently declined to diminish their profits by granting to their employees fair wages and decent conditions of employment; they find it cheaper to salve their consciences by a free bestowal of what is a misnomer to call 'charity'. . . . In these ways charity, as we understand it today, becomes identified with the maintenance of the existing social order and is consequently discredited in the eyes of all those who are striving to make democracy a reality, industrial and social, as well as political (Paulding, pp. 281–290).

Beyond the motives of the Charity Organization, many of its critics looked upon the process of the administration as being ineffective, dehumanizing and demoralizing. The preoccupation with eligibility often caused the agency to overlook those in need and led a clergyman to say in an address to the Cleveland Charity Organization Society: "I doubt as I read the New Testament whether the twelve disciples would have been able to qualify as worthy according to your system. And Christ himself might have been turned over by you to the police department as a vagrant without visible means of support" (Trattner, p. 84). Even if they were finally found eligible the length of the investigation would have caused the client hardship. George Washington Plunkitt of Tammany Hall said, "If a family is burned out . . . I don't refer them to the charity organization society, which would investigate their case in a month or two and decide that they were worthy of help about the same time they were dead from starvation" (Ibid., p. 86).

Mary Richmond's response was vigorous. She felt these criticisms were, at best, made in ignorance by people who had just begun to have contact with the poor. In cases like this the involved person tends to overreact and confront problems with intensity of emotion rather than scientific reason. In responding to the criticism that working people are not represented on boards of the Charity Organization Society, Richmond stated that rather than having snubbed labor leaders, they refused to be a part of the charity movement (Colcord & Mann, p. 46). In discussing the passion of social reform, Richmond belittled the intensity of social reformers and suggested that their reaction was the product of immaturity that, should they study the subject, they would return to scientific rationality (Ibid., pp. 47, 54–55).

Richmond looked upon her role as somewhere between the clerk who was preoccupied with details so that the general issues were overlooked, and the generalist whose passion for wholesale cures of the ills of society through legal reform denied her the ability to respect the work of the retail reformer. This retail reform is her concept of the middle ground. She compares it to the involvement that white participants in the underground railroad had with slaves. These relationships ultimately resulted in widespread sympathy with the cause of abolition. It was a person-to-person retail movement as opposed to political movements such as the Boston Anti-Slavery Society (Ibid., pp. 216–217). Because all people have an impact on a community, the changes in individuals would eventually have an impact on the broader community. Such change was the goal of the retail method of social reform. By a slow person-to-person approach attitudes would be changed, policies would be improved and the administration of programs be made more humane so that existing social structures could contend with social problems.

In later years Porter Lee, an associate of Mary Richmond, delineated the differences between the two types of social work: one was concerned with cause and the other was concerned with function. The social reformers of the wholesale type were those who addressed cause. Those who were individual casework types were interested in function. Although he stated that both were legitimate forms of the profession, his comments left no doubt about his sympathies. Lee (1930, pp. 3–20) delineated ten categories and specified the differences between each kind of social worker. He listed the purpose, motivation, leadership, appeal, justification, goals, basis for action, skills, organization and evaluation of the profession in the two kinds of practice. The cause people were characterized as zealots who addressed evil, were charismatic, appealed to the sentiments of the people, aroused the public through their conviction and leadership and functioned from a small informal base of support for a short period. In the end they had ony a crude sense of having accomplished their goals.

The function people, on the other hand, were "routineers" who were experts reaching for the intelligence of the people by informing them and appealing to their intelligence rather than their emotions. Their skills were studied and scientific rather than inspirational and they supposedly made scientific evaluations about the success of their efforts (see Spanos, pp. 7–8). There is little doubt which approach Lee held to be the appropriate one for the profession in spite of the apparent lack of support among social activists.

The settlement movement enjoyed a far greater degree of popular acceptance than the charity movement. They were generally not involved in the distribution of charity and therefore avoided the antipathy that the process created. There was the acceptance that concern for the poor and bringing culture to the slums were done by good workers. Finally, they were part of an open coalition with business people for reform and therefore part of the mainstream.

If there was an exception to this rule of cooperation between apparent adversaries, it was between the city bosses and settlement workers. It would be a fair assumption that the bosses' evaluations of the settlement workers was less than complimentary. The workers consistently attempted (almost always without success) to politically dislodge and discredit the bosses. With one exception, the bosses' views were lost to history because they were rarely written down. George Washington Plunkitt is the exception. While he does not relate directly to the settlement movement, he does speak about social reformers in general. In his study of Plunkitt, Riordon gives a record of the opinions of the colorful Tammany boss:

> [Lincoln] Steffens means well, but like all reformers, he don't know how to make distinctions. . . .
>
> There's the biggest kind of a difference between political looters and politicians who make a fortune out of politics by keeping their eyes open. The looter goes in for himself alone without considering his organization

or his city. The politician looks after his own interests, the organization's interests, and the city's interests all at the same time (p. 29).

Plunkitt maintains that these reformers always fail because they have not had the appropriate education in practical politics:

> I can't tell you how many of these movements I've seen started in New York during my forty years in politics, but I can tell you how many have lasted more than a few years—none. . . . They were morning glories—looked lovely in the morning and withered up in a short time, while the regular machines went on flourishing forever, like fine old oaks. . . .

> The fact is that a reformer can't last in politics. He can make a show for a while, but he always comes down like a rocket. . . . You've got to be trained up to [politics] or you're sure to fail. . . . [The reformer] hasn't been brought up in the difficult business of politics and he makes a mess of it every time (pp. 17, 19).

Jane Addams herself expresses insight by also taking the settlement movement to task. In an article almost mirroring some of Plunkitt's comments about the expertise of the ward politicians in relation to that of the settlement worker, she deals with the apparent frustration due to the lack of communication with clients (1898, pp. 6–9). She suggests that bosses develop an understanding and respect for the culture of those they serve. Their understanding of the values of their constituents enables them to assist them at times and in areas where the assistance is most appreciated by the recipient. It is in response to the needs that are felt by the people asking for the help.

The social workers, on the other hand, while they attempt to do good, relate to their own notions of helpfulness, reform and correctness. This, together with a lack of understanding of culture, adherence to rules and laws that are neither understood nor appreciated by the poor, and a bureaucracy that interferes with the administration of concrete services, made Jane Addams envious of the effectiveness of the word "boss" (Addams, 1898, pp. 6–9).

Unlike other reformers Addams recognized that the assumption that political bosses accumulated power and took bribes purely because of greed was more a reflection of these reformers' prejudices than the actual situation. What these reformers failed to see was that bossism was an important social system not just a reflection of the gullibility of ignorant immigrants. This system collected funds and encouraged political loyalty in order to maintain itself in power. In return, it distributed resources amongst its constituents and provided them with jobs.

The settlement people were also critical of their colleagues at the charity agencies. They echoed the critics of the labor unions and revealed the controversy and some of the antipathy that existed between the two branches of the profession.

The settlement workers tried to separate themselves from charity work even though they saw themselves as part of the same profession. They made efforts in the direction of attempting to promote certain professional ethical values. Settlement people saw themselves as friends of the poor living in their community rather than as outsiders dispensing charity.

Charity in Jane Addams' view was full of "don'ts" while settlement work concerned itself with "do's." They delivered services in terms of needs perceived by the poor, rather than concerning themselves with issues of eligibility:

> Jane Addams . . . felt that Charity Organization Society agents were cold and unemotional, too impersonal and stingy, that they were pervaded by a negative pseudoscientific spirit. Their vocabulary, she argued, was one of 'don't give,' 'don't act,' 'don't do this or that;' all they gave the poor was advice—and for that they probably sent the Almighty a bill (Trattner, p. 84).

In response the Charity Organization Society defined its actions as "effective" assistance. In their opinion the settlement movement was sentimental and vague, not knowing how to deal with the roots of poverty. Mary Richmond characterized the movement as having little focus and being so concerned with unmanagable diffuse issues that they rendered themselves generally ineffective. In fact, Richmond claimed that they may even cause the poor more harm than good, by inadvertently encouraging dependency (Colcord & Mann, pp. 121–122).

In the end, the differences between the charity organization and settlement movement, if not totally reconciled, were, at least, ignored. In the interest of professionalism they acknowledged each other's perceived contributions. Later they worked together to develop social work education. They merged their journals in 1905. In 1909 Jane Addams was elected President of the National Conference of Charities and Correction in spite of the fact that it was almost an arm of the Charity Organization Society. The movement also collaborated in forming the later National Conference of Social Welfare which is still in existence (Trattner, p. 149). Nonetheless the ideological conflict remained unsettled in the merged profession. The concern with the issue of the predominance of casework as over against social reform as the predominant focus of professional social work continues to be debated and remains a crucial issue in the field today.

Summary

The Progressive era at the turn of the century spawned a movement for political and business reform and programs to meet the needs of the poor. The people who had previously been engaged in the administration of charity became caught up in the developing programs and, together with settlement workers, emerged as a profession called social work. Under the leadership of such people as Mary Richmond, charity members of this new profession not only claimed to offer expertise in the efficient and fair administration of "scientific charity" but also claimed to have developed a process to permanently uplift the poor whom they served. Once identified, the problems could be attacked and solved through counseling, referral, environment manipulation, or advocating for the client. Their major thrust was toward issues and problems of an individual client or "retail" approach toward helping rather than societal reform or "wholesale" method.

Not all of the new profession held to the "retail" position. Jane Addams and her settlement house movement were vigorous participants in the movement for the overhaul of society. Their methodology was not tied to the granting of financial assistance. Rather they tried to improve conditions for the poor by becoming a part of their community, sharing their skills and education, and using whatever personal, economic and political resources they had for community improvement.

Although an alliance was struck between the two groups, the substance of the "wholesale" versus "retail" conflict was never resolved. Professional schools of social work developed out of this alliance and as a result the unresolved issue had a profound effect upon the character of the education process, as we shall see.

Chapter 3

The Theoretical Foundation of Social Work

The limits of practice and the goals of any profession are suggested by the particular knowledge base from which it draws its basic assumptions. Thus American medicine has developed certain characteristics because its knowledge base is in natural science. It differs from earlier European medicine based upon religious premises as well as forms of medicine practiced in China and the folk medicine of Africa which are also based upon premises other than natural science. Law, by the same token, has a theoretical foundation. It involves logic, history, political science and certain notions of justice and fairness. Education and social work practice are also reflections of their knowledge base.

As pointed out, the major premises under which social work education and practice operate are the result of a struggle between various schools of thought. In the most accurate sense social work never fully resolved the issue. There have even been times when the predominant position has yielded for a time to a minority view. These were temporary situations which gave way to one clear theoretical base emerging before 1930 and dominating the field. Since then, despite occasional variation, many of the original ideas for the profession came from a single source, the social casework movement. As the profession became an independent entity the Charity Organization Society and the settlement house movement developed theoretical postures that were a reflection of their positions in practice.

The settlement houses were inclined to retain the more global theoretical orientation of the allied fields of sociology, political science, and economics. The Charity Organization Society people, particularly Mary Richmond, spearheaded a rejection of these social sciences. Theirs was, as we pointed out, a narrower, more conservative perspective that spoke to an individual "rehabilitative" type of practice that came to be known as "casework." It was claimed that this was a more realistic perspective and it became the dominant view in social work.

The social worker needed experience in an agency rather than a deep understanding of theoretical material (Colcord and Mann, p. 90). Theory could be valuable so long as it lent itself to the development of technique and skills. Beyond that, theory was rejected as a time-consuming academic exercise without real value to the practitioner.

Sociology, it was felt, offered little guidance in developing techniques for working with individuals. The study of that subject was discouraged, therefore, because of its "inapplicability." Psychology seemed to serve that purpose better, because it usually included a technology of practice.

In the last analysis, however, all theory was secondary to the judgment of practitioners based upon practical experience. Casework, to the charity organization people, was atheoretical except where theory supported their preconceived notions. Both sociology and psychology were used to justify actions that were believed to be correct by the practitioners. Psychology, and later psychiatry, came to play a greater role in the knowledge base of social work because of their compatibility with the non-reform posture of the charity organization leadership of social work.

Charity and the Social Science Movement

Social work did not first exist and then choose a knowledge base; rather, it emerged from an academic area that developed in mid-nineteeth century American colleges and universities. This movement spawned not only social work, but also areas currently known as sociology, political science, economics, and social psychology.

The social science movement, originating in about 1840 (Bernard & Bernard, pp. 33–55), was an effort to unify the two ideas of social reform and science. Their initial philosophical base was liberal Christian theology. After 1850 they integrated the thoughts of Mills, Spencer, and Marx which had begun to take root during that period. In 1865, a group of Christian social science idealists from prominent families founded the American Social Science Association. Its stated initial purpose was the study of the causes and possible amelioration of society's ills. Most importantly, it felt that the basic tenets of science could be applied to the social order for its improvement.

The new association represented groups who were interested in a variety of disciplines within social science. Each interest group began to develop its own association within the parent organization. After a time, it divided itself into four sections: Education, Public Health,

Social Economy and Jurisprudence (Leiby, p. 95). Members of state boards of charity, as well as members of such organizations as the National Prison Association and Children's Aid Society (those involved in what we would now call social work), met as a part of the department of social economy.

As a result of the society's efforts, social science began to be introduced into the undergraduate curricula of some colleges and universities in the 1880s. The nature of the material taught was strongly oriented toward social reform. The religious foundation of the idealism of social science was reflected in the fact that courses were first taught in theological seminaries.

Social science courses were basically viewed as teaching theory in a new "science," with possible practical application. They were not, at first, considered professional training programs, although their content was considered useful for people who were engaged in philanthropic and correctional work. What was then called "sociology" included charity and community work. In fact, there was no explicit delineation of "charity" and "sociological" materials. The "sociology" label also included the areas of economics, political science, history, government and civics. The term "sociology" came to be used interchangeably with the term social science. The diversity of interests represented in the general category of social science and social science education led to conflict about the direction of the parent association. This ultimately resulted in the dissolution of the Social Science Association and the creation of various organizations representing the different disciplines.

The first organization to separate itself from the American Social Science Association was the group of people who were directly concerned with charity and correctional work. This phenomenon is surprising in that they were among the first who expressed an interest in the Association and were among its founders. The initial separation occurred in 1879 with the formation of the National Conference of Charities and Corrections. On a deeper level this move exemplified the move away from the social reform perspective of the social sciences.

In 1876 the Wisconsin charity delegation of the American Social Science Association expressed concern about the general policy of the organization to deal with matters of theory. They preferred a greater emphasis upon practice. The next year, in 1877, this Wisconsin group became so concerned that it indicated that it would not send a delegation to the 1878 meeting. It introduced the idea that a separate organization for *practical* social science was needed. The separate Conference of Charities and Corrections was formed at that time. The first meeting of this new association as an independent entity was in 1879 (Broadhurst, pp. 75–90).

This move by the social workers seemed to herald the ultimate disintegration of the association. Other interest groups soon began following suit and formed their own independent organizations. The American Historical Association was founded in 1884, the American Economic Association in 1885, the American Political Science Association in 1904 and the American Sociological Association in 1905. The American Social Science Association dissolved in 1909.

The National Conference of Charities and Corrections was an instant success. The attendance at the first meeting in 1879 surpassed the hopes of the founders. It suggested that many of the members worked and lobbied for the actions of the Wisconsin delegation. In addition, the speed with which the change occurred seemed to indicate that the separation was not entirely unexpected. Nonetheless, many of the people involved in the action retained their membership in both organizations.

The people who joined both associations considered themselves part of a single discipline called either social science or sociology. When in 1909 the old Social Science Association finally dissolved, the National Conference of Charities and Corrections claimed to attempt to incorporate the sociological theoretical component within its objectives. However, except for an occasional mention of theory, the organization remained almost completely concerned with practice.

The estrangement of the practitioners from the association was not only the social workers' doing. Those who represented the theoretical side of social science did little to oppose the movement of charity and corrections work away from sociology.

Social scientists also were said to feel that very little of social work was of use to them and that their material was not based upon "scientific" data. It is thus not difficult to understand why there was so little resistance by them to the social workers' leaving the American Social Science Association. Social work gave lip service to sociology as its knowledge base for a long time in spite of the separation. However, there was growing discontent with this relationship, particularly among social workers who were part of the charity organization society movement. This discontent eventually resulted in a complete schism between social work and sociology.

Social Work Rejects a Sociological Knowledge Base

During the beginning of the formation of the National Association of Charities and Corrections the practitioners accepted a sociological knowledge base but seemed to have no clear idea of what benefit social work actually accrued from sociology. From the beginning some social workers expressed real antagonism toward sociology. The most vociferous of these objections came from the Charity Organization Society.

Other powerful social workers throughout the literature made constant reference to the inapplicability of sociology. Early in the history of the International Congress of Charities Correction and Philanthropy in 1893 a social work leader indicated that he was distressed that the conference was entitled "Sociology in Institutions of Learning." He suggested that his interest was *only* in philanthropy, a much narrower and in many ways a different field than sociology. He therefore proposed a specific identification of social science that related to his concerns and the concerns of other philanthropists and he proposed that this particular field be identified as "Philanthropology" (Warner, pp. 80–92).

Porter Lee, the general secretary of the Philadelphia Charity Organization Society, 1909–1912, was another example of the social work opposition (Hellenbrand, pp. 13–14). He commented to a questionnaire about the relationship of sociology to social work that his studies in sociology were "interesting" and "profitable," but no more so than the New Testament or Wells' *Outline of History*. Lee was an extremely powerful member of the social work profession. Not only did he represent the Charity Organization Society, but his opinions played an important role in the development of social work education. He became a teacher in the New York School of Social Work in 1909. After serving three years in that capacity, he went on to become the director of this prestigious school and remained at that post until 1938 (Meier, pp. 141–42).

The antipathy that developed between social work and sociology continued to simmer throughout the 1920s. The two fields had moved from their common ground to a condition of antagonism, distrust and a consensus that the content of each was irrelevant to the other. Time after time social work articles appeared citing opinions and studies reaffirming the inadequacy of sociology as a knowledge base for social work.

A 1919 paper maintained that social work and sociology were both concerned with standards, customs and tradition but in different ways. The author maintained that social work was concerned with maintenance and reestablishment of social standards in certain individual cases. On the other hand, sociology addressed not only the development of social structures but also tried to show what aspects of social structure could be modified. In his mind such active participation in social changes was not properly in the province of social work (Chapin, pp. 358–365).

The definitive study of social work education of its time states:

> . . . the criticism directed upon sociology is that it is content to attach a name to a problem, generalize about it, and then pass it up. The social worker who eagerly awaits suggestions to be developed into a technique of treatment finds this very unpalatable (Walker, pp. 184–85).

It is very difficult to find arguments fully in support of sociology after the 1920s. The best that can be found are suggestions that the subject may indeed be valuable for a broad understanding of human behavior. However, the subject is always found wanting in the area of applicability.

Perhaps the most evident area where sociology was rejected was in social work education. In the first important full-scale study of social work education Charles Tufts called for a sociological knowledge base to be taught in the schools of social work. In addition, the importance of teaching theories of all kinds was emphasized in the report. The depth of feeling this study created can be illustrated by the reaction of Jeffery Brackett, the dean of the new Boston School of Social Work. In a memorandum, he expressed dismay suggesting that the study left things "unsettled." He went on to suggest that the study should be withheld from publication. Instead it could be printed in paper covers and circulated only privately. Fortunately for the history of social work education, Brackett failed and this important study was published (Levy, p. 35).

That the recommendations of Tufts had little or no effect can be demonstrated by the reaction of the schools in terms of their actual curricula and entrance requirements during the 1920s when curriculum content became institutionalized. Jesse Frederick Steiner reported that:

> When . . . entrance requirements (of social work schools) are subjected to another test of a graduate school, namely, insistence upon preprofessional studies that would give the students a knowledge of the sciences related to their field of work, an equally unsatisfactory showing is made. In general, the value of preliminary instruction in the social sciences is recognized but such instruction is not made an absolute requirement. In their references to such subjects the bulletins usually adopt such phrases as "familiarity is recommended" or, "a desirable preparation" instead of recognizing that technical instruction in social work must be based on a knowledge of the social sciences (Steiner, pp. 34–35).

The study continued with specifics as to the lack of social science entrance requirements at these new schools of social work. The Richmond School of Social Work at William and Mary made no mention about the desirability of knowledge of the social sciences in its statement of requirements. The New York, Boston and Chicago schools also did not include sociology in the list of studies mentioned as desirable preparation for their program.

Ten years after the Steiner work, Karpf made a detailed study of every social work curriculum in the United States. He reported every course in every program. In spite of the fact that his work quotes many social work leaders who endorse social science as valuable for social workers, the programs did not reflect that. In the survey of all twenty-eight of the schools in existence at that time only one school was shown to offer a course in sociology called "Clinical Sociology." Two other schools offered courses in "Social Psychology of Leadership" and "Government and Social Work." They were likewise isolated, single-semester courses. In contrast, all schools offered elaborate two-year programs in material that was oriented toward casework practice. These courses included agency material to which psychological material was applied (Karpf, p. 330).

Thus by 1931 social science was no longer a significant part of social work education. Where theory was taught it tended to be psychological in nature. By 1930 the basic structure of social work education became institutionalized. The casework and psychological content remained central up until the present time. As will be demonstrated in later chapters even the needs of the field during the crisis periods of the 1930s and 1960s failed to be reflected in social work education. The appeals for "relevant content," i.e., more global than casework, by practitioners in the public welfare sector were common but futile. Social work suffered an enormous loss of credibility because of the inability of the schools to prepare practitioners to meet the challenges of the times. In the end it was the narrowness of the accepted casework/psychological model that did not provide the content needed to develop the required practice skills.

The stubbornness with which the field clung to the rejection of social science, therefore, seems to require an explanation beyond the one offered by social workers that these subjects did not offer a base for practice. We will examine three possible underlying reasons for the disregard of sociology and related fields. The first of these will be the claim that sociology and related subjects were politically incompatible with the needs of the philanthropists that supported social workers and social agencies. We shall also consider the jurisdictional dispute for control of social work education between social science theorists and social work practitioners. Finally, we must consider the development of measures of accountability and empirical testing within the social sciences. These tests threatened the premises of social work programs. By rejecting social science, social workers limited their responsibility to subject themselves to these measures of credibility.

From the beginning of the American Social Science Association, many of the social science leaders took the opposite view, i.e., there needed to be change in society as a whole. They did encourage social activism and threaten the established order. The financial support of social work, particularly the Charity Organization Societies, came from people such as Morgan, Carnegie and others who were the established order. They made up the governing boards of these agencies and in some cases were involved directly in their administration and sometimes even acted as volunteers in providing direct services. They were very influential.

The content of social science spoke to the redistribution of wealth, the unfair advantages of the privileged, the need for a classless society, and explored the interaction between people that allowed for the continuation of society without change. Many social scientists looked for ways to upset the existing balance. The knowledge drawn from social science about the structure of society in the hands of social workers whose lives were devoted toward bettering conditions for people who were disadvantaged must have been perceived by philanthropists as dangerous. This could explain why the Charity Organization Society acted to encourage distance between the two fields.

Social work's relationship to the Johns Hopkins University provides an interesting study of the perception of one philanthropist toward sociologically oriented social work. In his inaugural address as president of the new university in 1876, Daniel Gillman dedicated himself and his school to the betterment of society. Prior to beoming president, Dr. Gillman was a founder of the most important and powerful Charity Organization Society in the United States, the Baltimore Charity Organization Society. It was the Charity Organization Society where Mary Richmond had built her professional reputation.

Only one year after the founding of Johns Hopkins, a strong faculty in sociology had been established. Yet, although the school had committed itself so completely to social science and to providing professionals to function within society, no school of social work was founded. This was in spite of the fact that the first place Mary Richmond attempted to form a school of social work was at Johns Hopkins.

In 1878, President Gillman openly expressed the fear that the inclination toward "agitation" of the American Association of Social Science might "be confused with scholarship" (Broadhurst, p. 386). President Gillman was able to keep the theories of planned social change out of the hands of the practitioners. In doing so he reflected some of the attitudes of wealthy business people about social science. Business interests that welcomed the advantages provided to them by biological and physical science eschewed the social sciences:

> . . . the rising industrialists, who profited from the application of science to industry, were not opposed to science as such. They generally favored the exact sciences which brought the new inventions and more wealth. They were opposed only to social sciences, or human science, which, they clearly perceived, threatened their earnings in the name of a more just distribution of wealth and operated in behalf of a newly organized and more democratic social order. These men also identified social science with social reform and hated the former because they dreaded the latter (Bernard & Bernard, p. 55).

The aversion of business people who supported social agencies to social science is only part of the reason given for the separation of sociology and social work. Other issues were also involved. One such issue was the control of schools of social work. The social workers who pressed for professional education perceived its content to be practical material derived from the experience of agencies. This need for social work education to be controlled by the practitioners led to the rejection of theory.

Another point of contention between social work and sociology was the fact that social scientists were beginning to study some of the basic premises of established charity work. These studies often questioned the validity and effect of charity organizations' efforts. For example, Richard Ely began to scrutinize the statistics of the Charity Organization Society caseload. He was able to point out that, although the prevention of pauperism was presented as the major part of the agency's effort, paupers, in a true sense, represented a ridiculously low percentage of their caseload (Broadhurst, pp. 775–777).

The reaction of social workers to such an evaluation was understandably defensive. To them the defect could be found in the research method, not in social work practice. Mary Richmond expressed concern about the appropriateness of such studies to social work. She claimed that social investigation was a laboratory method of study. An equally scientific method that would be, in her opinion, more valid for the practice of social work could be the "clinical or case method." She delineated the two methods:

Social research deals with masses, case inquiry and units. The one is extensive and the other intensive. The besetting sin of the one is the fallacy of averages, of the other the fallacy of the individual instance (Colcord & Mann, p. 311).

While Richmond states that she sees both as valid methods, the clinical method is preferred. The "fallacy of the individual instance" could be used to eschew the results of studies that were uncomfortable for those who had a vested interest in existing procedures and policy. Without research to test effectiveness, programs and the methods employed were not subject to empirical accountability.

These difficulties required rejection of the sociological foundation. A new theory needed to be formulated. Mary Richmond set about taking on this awesome task.

Charity Organization Theory for Casework Practice

The method practiced by the Charity Organization Society came to be known as casework. This method started as an investigation of clients in order to determine eligibility for financial assistance and to uncover fraud. It quickly branched out and claimed to deal with the personal difficulties that allegedly grew out of poverty and unscientifically administered charity: dependency, vagrancy and pauperism. In the absence of empirical evidence the goals and methods of casework could be justified with testimonials and case examples. Theories of various types could be chosen from one area or another to legitimate procedures that had already been decided upon by caseworkers. "Common sense" notions of practitioners were then added to form a theory structure upon which further practice was based. Casework practice had, in short, become its own theoretical foundation. Sociology, because of its social action component, did not suit this purpose. The field moved to areas that were more compatible with casework practice. This moved casework to become more and more involved in the use of selected psychological material, particularly in clinical areas. This process can be illustrated by the development of the casework alternative.

The Charity Organization Society originally defined itself as a vehicle to coordinate charity agencies so that grants and services would be given only to the deserving poor. Those who could work would be sorted out by the agency. In addition, the coordination would provide lists of recipients from each agency to prevent duplication of assistance. These ends would be accomplished through a thorough investigation. The purpose of the agency was to serve the philanthropist's interests through the efficient use of his generosity.

From this perspective it is easy to understand how the agency quickly became involved in actions of a broader scope that also served the interests of wealthy philanthropists. This interaction can be illustrated by a Charity Organization Society action involving vagrancy in Buffalo, New York.

The suppression of tramps during the depression of 1892–1894 in Buffalo, New York shows such interaction (Harring, pp. 876–893). Because there was a promise of work, previously working poor gathered in this city. The promise failed to materialize and these "tramps" remained. At first, efforts were made to provide some assistance to these men. However, with the encouragement of business groups, police were turned against the tramps and the Charity Organization Society discontinued their efforts, labeling the hoboes "thieves." The Charity Organization Society played an active role in supporting legislation to suppress these unemployed men known as the "Tramp Act." This law provided for imprisonment of vagrants and for recourse to police assistance to remove them from the community. The Charity Organization Society actively supported police actions during the crisis and the vigorous enforcement of the Tramp Act.

Beyond such actions, the organization sought to become involved in what it viewed as the full spectrum of the causes of poverty. Subjective poverty had the characteristics of indolence, disease, lack of judgment, and unhealthy appetite. These were said to be caused by certain habits such as shiftlessness, self-abuse and sexual excess, abuse of narcotics, unhealthy diet, and disregard of family ties.

"Objective" causes involved such factors as inadequate natural resources, bad climatic conditions, defective sanitation, evil associations in surroundings, misdirected or inadequate education and bad industrial conditions. Also included was unwise philanthropy that was assumed to encourage dependency (Warner, pp. 183–201).

While casework qua "friendly visiting" had been practiced from the beginning of the Charity Organization Societies, it was Mary Richmond who codified it into a genuine method of practice. This codification came about for two reasons. First, the field had been dependent for a long time on volunteers. Professionalization had been a major concern of the Charity Organization Society workers who were now being paid. They suggested that the abuses of clients' rights had come about through the insensitivity of volunteers. Professionalism instead of volunteerism was a way to avoid this.

While Richmond retained allegiance to the volunteer system, acceptance of the professionalization argument provided an excellent medium for the second important reason for her work, meeting the organizational needs of the Charity Organization Society. A professional methodology could be used to justify perceptions and activities of the organization. Since the Charity Organization Society had been criticized as being repressive to the poor, Richmond's efforts were widely accepted.

Richmond's theory borrowed heavily from the medical model. She defined four processes that constituted the casework technique: insight into the personality, insight into the environment, action to produce personal rehabilitation which she called direct action, and indirect action which was an intervention in the environment (Lubove, p. 48). In short, the first two elements constituted diagnosis, and the second two, treatment. The diagnostic aspect was the one given the most attention by Richmond. She also favored the direct treatment method, i.e., rehabilitation. In the long run, this minimized the desirability of relief or other tangible assistance because it was said that, unlike rehabilitation, it did not address itself to the root causes of poverty and encouraged ongoing dependency (Ibid., p. 52).

To Mary Richmond the concept of diagnosis in the medical sense was extremely relevant to the social work process (Richmond, 1917, pp. 52–55). In social work, as in medicine, a pathogen, a hidden evil, could be "diagnosed" and attacked through treatment so that the disease it caused could be alleviated. Diagnosis was a continuing process that could be modified as conditions changed for the patient.

In her definitive work on diagnosis, *Social Diagnosis*, Richmond defines the concept in the following way:

> Social diagnosis, then, may be described as the attempt to make as exact a definition as possible of the situation and personality of a human being in some social need—of his situation and personality, that is, in relation to the other human beings upon whom he in any way depends or depend on him, and in relation also to the social institutions of his community (p. 357).

Social Diagnosis goes beyond the simple definition of problem areas. Within her book, Richmond delineates the process for gathering the information necessary for the diagnosis. She also presents a codification and even elements of a nomenclature of factors to be examined.

This careful treatment of the process sets up a complex quasi-scientific method, that, according to Richmond, requires skill and training to implement. The skilled practitioner of social diagnosis would be able to identify hidden problem areas requiring treatment that would not be apparent to the layman. The process was seen as parallel to the way a physician could identify illness in a person who looked normal to the untrained.

Thus, Richmond developed the notion that the field had become too complex to be staffed by volunteers. The skills involved intense training that could be given to those who were willing to give their full attention to developing their ability. Volunteers were useful but only under the supervision of such a professional. This argument eventually led to the development of long periods of agency training for new workers and ultimately to the push for professional schools.

In addition to the identification of the problem areas Richmond and other charity people developed a process that would help clients rehabilitate themselves from poverty and its effects. This process was called, at first, "Friendly Visiting." The program was designed to see the "immaterial" needs of clients while grants were administered to meet their "material" needs (Richmond, 1899). Together with the preference for "retail reform," a case-by-case involvement in social change rather than more global "wholesale reform," Richmond's casework took on an individually oriented psychological character:

> Social casework consists of those processes which develop personality through adjustment, consciously effected, individual by individual, between men and their environment (Richmond, 1922, pp. 98–99).

The social environment is not eliminated from Richmond's model. She states that casework is also ". . . development of personality through the conscious and comprehensive adjustment of social relationships" (Ibid., p. 98). This definition places the world of the client within the jurisdiction of the caseworker. The power exercised by the caseworker is enhanced by the position he or she holds because of his or her professional expertise.

Because the social worker was a professional, Richmond felt that his or her decision making took precedence over the client's legal rights. This was particularly true in juvenile court and child welfare, where the social worker's knowledge would facilitate the early identification of problems. In addition, if heeded, casework treatment recommendations would assist the court in setting right the client's difficulties.

It was argued, for example, that rules of evidence were designed to meet the needs of a court that depended upon lay people to make decisions. "Social Evidence," Richmond's name for information acquired through social diagnosis by an expert social worker, belonged in the decision-making process. The high degree of reliability assured by the professional should allow the court to relax the rigidity of the rules

of evidence, particularly when the best interests of a child or other
person needing special protection as perceived by the caseworker were
being served. Thus the court would benefit from the work of social
workers by being able to take more efficient action:

> . . . no considerable group of social caseworkers—whether in a society to
> protect children or a charity organization or anywhere else—seem to
> have grasped the fact that the *reliability* of the evidence on which they
> base their decisions should be no less rigidly scrutinized than that of
> legal evidence by opposing counsel. . . . Social evidence, like that sought
> by the scientist or historian, includes all items which, however trifling or
> apparently irrelevant when regarded as isolated facts, may, when taken
> together, throw light upon the question at issue; namely as regards social
> work, the question of what courses of procedure will place this client in
> his right relation to society (Richmond, 1917, p. 39).

To illustrate the point, Richmond indexes social evidence as over
against legal evidence so that they can be contrasted:

Social Evidence	*Reason why. . . .the Court Would Not Act*
This family has lived in two tiny rooms on the top floor. Although their tenement rooms are sunny and clean, the children do not get sufficient exercise or air. The parents refuse to move as the rent is small.	The sunniness of the tenement and the fact that the mother keeps it clean would prevent a court from regarding these cramped quarters as evidence of culpable neglect. Public opinion would not uphold the court in making an issue of home conditions that were not considerably below the ideal held by social workers . . . .
A year and a half after having been urged to have the two younger children examined, the mother took the youngest child to the hospital and promised to bring the second child. Eight months later she had not done this.	While it looks as if the family had been neglected in years past either deliberately or through ignorance, or both, the situation today is not clear. The oldest child is still in the hospital, the youngest has received hospital care, and the mother has promised to take the second child to the outpatient department. With this evidence of good intentions, a doctor's statement would be necessary to satisfy a court of present neglect (Ibid., p. 46).

It is clear from the foregoing that a social worker's expertise was considered sufficient to override the judgment of parents. Furthermore, the inability of the courts to force parents to take the actions deemed appropriate by the social worker was looked upon as a failure of the system to act in the best interest of children and to punish what was viewed as culpable neglect. Rather than attacking social injustice, the "social" aspect of social work, in many ways, had become the most repressive and intrusive facet of practice. Another school of casework functionalism saw the need for a new theory not encumbered by these social concerns.

Functionalist Casework Theory

Functionalism, a later form of casework developed by Virginia Robinson, discarded involvement in the social world of the client almost entirely (Robinson, 1930). Robinson's interpretation of the history of casework was that it represented a gradual movement away from environmental concerns and toward a thorough involvement in the client's intrapsychic functioning. The first period of casework was seen as its "sociological" period. It was, in Robinson's view, followed by the more psychologically oriented material of Mary Richmond's *Social Diagnosis*. Richmond's approach was seen as an intermediate step which was now being succeeded by the new functional method, an ethical move away from repression because it was less "sociological" (Robinson, 1930, pp. 66"7).

Also rejected was psychoanalysis as a basis for practice particularly as it related to diagnosis. Just as had been the case with sociology, the functionalists defined the theory in such a way as to lend itself suitable to functionalist criticism (Ibid., pp. 33–37). Instead, the "Will Psychology" of Otto Rank was seen as the theoretical underpinning of the functional movement. While the functional perspective on Freudianism was rejected by most caseworkers, the position on social reform became generally accepted.

Social reform was seen as too burdensome and irrelevant to the major objective of casework and the improvement of the lot of the individual. Concern for such global issues took time and other limited resources away from this major task of social work. These concerns were more within the realm of the general area that should be reserved for those involved in government. Social workers needed to limit themselves to the application of these general rules to the specifics of the individual case. It was in this area that they had their expertise.

Robinson reiterated the point and expressed the feeling that social work did not receive the understanding from others because of its involvement in social reform issues in addition to individual therapy:

> I believe that this recognition of the contribution of social work can only be established if the profession of social work can separate itself from its identification with the social conscience and social reform and find a role for itself in a more limited and more effective relation to social problems (Robinson, 1942, p. 11).

The social and individual worlds are viewed as separate and conflicting. The practictioner was seen as being unable to effectively participate professionally in both.

> This struggle of opposing tendencies, together constituting an unbroken trend in time, is the struggle between the individual and social, the one and the many, the psychological and the economic, the inner experience and the external event . . . leadership in social work has flourished through individuals who have carried with passionate devotion either one side or the other of this conflict (Faatz, p. 10).

The professional with his or her contact with the poor and other troubled groups should indeed have a special knowledge of social needs. If social workers become involved, these needs should be expressed by specialists in community organization whose sole interest is in social reform. Caseworkers because of their interest in the individual must exercise their expertise in political and social activities outside of their jobs. In this way they will positively affect the "social will" of the community with their expert knowledge without forcing their view upon others through their agency. In fact, professional involvement in social action could be viewed as an imposition of a presumptuous professional of his or her positions upon the community. This would be an interference with the community's right to come to its own conclusions.

The agency also was presented as having a limited role. Both the worker and the client needed to accept this role as they chose to work or seek help at a particular agency (Robinson, 1942, p. 13; Faatz, pp. 60–61). Thus the limited nature of the involvement of agencies and workers in social activism was enforced by this notion. The worker engaging in reform activities perhaps needed to reconsider his or her vocational choice and to make a change.

The Rankian psychology that formed the basis of the therapeutic theory was strongly oriented toward the intrapsychic life. The client was dealt with in terms of his or her life at the time of therapy. The detailed historical and social information garnered by caseworkers in the psychoanalytic or psychiatric fields at the time was seen as unnecessary. Mary Richmond and her followers were referred to as the "Diagnostic School" by the functionalists.

Rather than diagnosis the major focus of treatment was the establishment of a relationship in functionalism. Only diagnosis useful in the actual delivery of a specific service was relevant. Diagnosis tended to predetermine therapy while the development of a functional therapeutic process related to a client's needs as the client entered and progressed through the relationship (Smalley, pp. 80–81).

The client was said to have a will toward the actualization of his or her identity. Difficulty arose for clients when they were unable or unwilling to make decisions that would move them toward meeting their needs. The casework relationship was a medium whereby the client could be freed from the difficulties that prevented him or her from making the necessary choices and taking the necessary actions to reach fulfillment. Thus functional casework, unlike "Freudian" casework, served to reestablish normal functioning without the assumption of grave underlying illness or the necessity for disassembling the personality.

The process of developing the ability to use the relationship was complicated by resistance, a part of every client's life. The warmth and understanding created by the skilled worker served to alleviate this factor over time. What was essential was for the worker to be careful not to impose his or her will upon the client. This would serve to increase resistance and would not achieve the goals of therapy. Instead, the initiative of the client in his or her own problem-solving needed to be encouraged. In short, the worker needed to control the relationship so that such freedom could exist without imposing direction upon the client. In an environmental conflict the client would be freed to take action himself or herself rather than have access to a social work advocate.

The professional needed a great deal of training in order to perform this complex process. The functionalists concentrated in the school of social work at the University of Pennsylvania and, in the main considered themselves a separate school of thought. The training that they offered became known as the most rigid and controlling. The resistance assumed to be a part of the client's role in therapy was also seen as part of the student's role. Students needed to make a decision to "use" help. Those who "resisted" too much were seen as needing to reconsider their choice of school or profession. Resistance often amounted to questioning the shiboleths of the school, including the therapeutic model, or the apparent passive nature of functional casework. The educational process, rather than attempting to stimulate a challenging mind, used its sanctioning powers to repress it to the extreme. Education was defined as a process that went through three phases: fight, yield, and grow. One former Pennsylvania student related that his colleagues abbreviated the three phases as the acronym "fyg." When the students had finally given in to the pressure to conform they were said to have been "fyged" (Kraft, 1980, personal contact).

The introduction of functionalism created conflict in the social work profession. Criticism came from the "diagnostic" clinicians as well as those social workers who favored an activist approach (Hollis & Taylor, pp. 32–34).

The clinical reaction to functionalism was at first to accept, but antipathy grew as the conflict gained in momentum. The argument had to do with technique in the casework relationship. The intensity of the fight is reflected in Reynold's comments:

> By 1952, the practical repercussions of the conflict were so serious that agencies were labeled either diagnostic or functional, and there was difficulty in referring clients between the two. Schools were not placing students for field work in agencies of the wrong "faith." Applicants for employment were asked to which school they belonged and were not considered by some agencies if they said, "To neither" (1963, pp. 284–285).

The activists were quicker in their recognition of the implications of functionalism. Lurie expressed consternation that Robinson, in her initial book, had attempted to change the shape of social work practice. He suggested that the approach was mystical and atomistic. It did not take into consideration the economic depression that was going on at the time that *A Changing Psychology in Social Casework* was published. Rather, it led agencies away from social issues and toward dealing with "relationships" (Lurie, pp. 488–89).

In the end the field reacted to functionalism as if it were, in Reynolds' terms, "an earthquake" (Reynolds, 1931, pp. 111–14). In the clinical area Robinson's effect was no more than a whimper. The field had begun to align itself with the mental hygiene movement in the area of Psychiatric Social Work. People within this specialty were more inclined to accept a more conventional psychiatric perspective (this became particularly evident during the development of the curriculum and will be considered in detail in the chapter that deals with that issue). Rankian notions were fought with ferocity by those people in order to prevent them from permeating casework.

The effects of functionalism was most strongly felt in the social reform arena. Here the views of the functionalists matched those of conservative clinicians. Therefore, there was a much wider acceptance of this stance, than there had been of the clinical views. In addition, the controlling aspects of functional treatment and education seemed to catch on in the field. Thus the major effect of functionalism was in the area justifying the move of the field away from social reform, and the intensity and rigidity with which caseworkers exercised their control over students and clients.

Summary

The presentation of the development of the knowledge base of social work in this chapter was made to illustrate how this aspect was a reflection of the direction that the profession was to take. The most important of these effects was the fact that the rejection of the social science knowledge base moved the field away from social activism. This activism was seen as incipient in social science by social workers and the philanthropists who supported their agencies. Moving the practitioners away from such a knowledge base alleviated the threat that they would become involved in implementing reforms suggested by social science theory.

Also of concern to social workers was the control of social work education. If they retained their relationship with the social science theorists, the practitioners would have to yield control of the curriculum of the social work schools to the theorists who were academicians. The schools were viewed as the product of the efforts of practitioners, thereby satisfying the need for training people in practice technique. Thus, distance between social workers and academic theorists was viewed as serving the independent control of social work education by practice people.

Sociology had begun to develop empirical tests that raised issue about the credibility of the assumptions and practice of casework. Remaining in the social science field meant being accountable to the results of this empirical evidence. Separation reduced this risk.

When social casework moved away from the social science knowledge base, it left a vacuum. The field needed some way to justify practice. Mary Richmond developed a codification of the field that served this purpose. She borrowed from a variety of theoretical areas in her model of "casework theory." Two areas that were particularly important were medicine and psychology. Medicine was the foundation of the theory of practice. Social problems were viewed as pathogens that needed to be diagnosed and treated by the expert professional social worker. The effort was geared to equate the expertise of the social worker with that of the physician. Such a parallel would give the profession the respect and the decision-making power that Richmond thought it ought to have. What it created was the view of the client as a patient whose troubles emanated from an internal illness rather than external environmental problems. Further it justified casework practice that was presumptuous, intrusive, controlling and often repressive.

The emphasis upon an internal source of client problems made a psychological knowledge base more attractive than a social science one. Richmond stressed rehabilitative counseling as her treatment of choice. Psychology provided, in her mind, the skills with which to implement such treatment. As the field adopted this knowledge more and more it moved further and further away from coping with social problems through global social reform. Thus a psychological orientation of the field tended to minimize its involvement in social activism.

The psychological bent gained widespread support in the field. It ultimately resulted in a specialization in social work, "Psychiatric Social Work," as well as a psychiatric orientation in other casework areas. An extreme example of this clinical orientation was the branch of social work that was known as functionalism. This was an extremely conservative form of casework that attempted to adapt the theory of Otto Rank to casework practice. It was a theory that not only explained peoples' problems as being totally psychological but advocated a completely passive role for the caseworker in the client's social environment. By the same token the caseworker was extremely controlling in his or her relationship with the client. In keeping with this, functionalism completely rejected a social reform role for the caseworker. While social work practice rejected the clinical theory of the functionalists, the control, acceptance of psychology, and the resultant rejection of social reform advocated by them were accepted more widely by the field.

This rejection of theory oriented toward social reform, together with the jurisdictional concerns between academicians and practitioners for control of social work education, created problems for the creation of the schools of social work, as we shall see.

Chapter 4

The Affiliation Question in Social Work Education

Soon after the American Social Science Association was formed, first divinity schools and then universities began to include social science information in their curricula. The force behind the acceptance of this content were members of the Association who also became the first teachers of the material. They were well educated, idealistic and often wealthy people with status in the academic community. Many of these people later became closely involved with the settlement movement, the liberal wing of social work.

While these programs were developing, a large group of people were engaged in the practice of social work in the Charity Organization Societies, child saving agencies, prisons, and other institutions. In many cases they were not as well educated and had come to social work primarily to earn a salary rather than to perform tasks that would achieve ideological goals. The conflict between the two groups resulted in the dissolution of the Association and abandonment of a sociological knowledge base, as already discussed. It also played a significant role in the creation of schools of social work.

This conflict manifested itself most clearly in the decision over whether to affiliate the professional schools with universities. It represented a jurisdictional dispute about who would control the education of practitioners: the academic liberals or the more conservative practitioners.

Although the early curricula in social science were filled with practice content, they were rejected by the practitioners as too theoretical. The practitioners called for schools of social work that were independent of university programs. Their success, even though it was only partial and temporary, had the effect of moving professional education in social work away from an idealistic social reform perspective toward a technique-oriented personal, rehabilitative, helping approach.

We must therefore look at the jurisdictional dispute that revolved around the affiliation issue. We will look at the early social science programs, the nature of the call for independent schools of social work, the schools that resulted from this effort, and the controversies that characterized the struggle for control of social work education in these early programs. Finally, we examine here the pressures that lead to the reconciliation of the issue on the formation of schools of social work that affiliated with universities as graduate schools.

Early Programs of Social Work Education

The first school to teach sociology was Harvard Divinity School in 1880. The course was called "Social Ethics" and was considered by many to have inspired the theological sociology courses that were later to be offered at other seminaries (Brackett, pp. 160–161).

Sociology found its way into the newer secular schools at about the same time. In 1884 Cornell offered the first secular sociology course. By 1887 Johns Hopkins boasted of having three of the best sociologists in the country on its faculty (Broadhurst, p. 386). An 1893 report indicated that by that time a dozen colleges offered systematic instruction in sociology, including Harvard, Brown, Columbia, Johns Hopkins, Chicago, Stanford and the State Universities of Iowa, Wisconsin, Kansas, and Minnesota. The nature of the courses being offered clearly indicated the fact that social work-like activities were very much a part of what was called sociology at that time.

Many of these courses had a component built into them which was called field study. Here the students were asked to enter the community and observe, as well as attempt to influence, the various social problems addressed by the courses. The development of laboratories in these courses created the impetus that eventually led to the beginning of what became American settlement houses (Taylor, pp. 72–73).

The content of the courses in sociology covered the full gamut of concerns in the applied social sciences. Yet to many practitioners the programs were said to have real deficiencies for people who were employed in the giving of direct services. The existing programs were, in their view, too preoccupied with theory and did not address themselves to technical considerations. Furthermore, these courses were expensive and part of a liberal arts college education that was available to very few people at the time. Charity and correction workers were usually not college educated and did not see formal education as essential to their work. What they required was training in the skills of their practice that would be helpful in dealing with the day-to-day problems they faced on the job (Dawes, pp. 14–20).

Very little effort was made to approach existing educational programs to request changes that would satisfy the practitioners. Instead, their proposals involved the creation of a separate group of training programs that would be specific to practice and practitioners. To those involved in the administration of charity, the transmission of skills, rather than speculation about society's obligations to the poor, needed to be the object of professional training. Schools that were separate from universities and under the control and administration of practitioners and their agencies were said to fill such a need.

The Call for Professional Schools

The first charity worker to make an appeal for an independent professional school was Anna Dawes. She addressed the National Conference of Charities and Corrections in 1893. Her argument gave a clear picture of the split in backgrounds and goals between the practice and theory people. Dawes pointed to low salaries in social work and suggested two groups of people who would be willing to work for so little money: "those who were college educated and functioned from a missionary impulse and the majority of practitioners, . . . that large class of able and efficient young men and women who without other than a public school education are satisfied, at least temporarily, with such a salary as I have named" (Ibid., p. 16).

The programs that Dawes suggested were aimed at people who were not from colleges and needed some way of developing the skills required for their jobs. People in universities could not be depended upon to provide the necessary training. Their thought processes were far too theoretical and did not relate to the practical work of charity (Levy, p. 15). Her argument was that those who taught in universities were unable to understand the details of everyday living. College-educated people, furthermore, demanded a high salary and were not as willing to work in small communities where the need for new charity workers was greatest. Thus college programs needed to be replaced by training schools whose programs would be:

> . . . made under such auspices and should cover so brief a period, should be superficial if you choose to say so, that it need not be unduly expensive, for the *sine qua non* of this profession is the possibility of procuring trained workers for a moderate salary (Dawes, pp. 18–19).

In 1897 Mary Richmond resurrected the Dawes plan in a paper delivered at the National Conference of Charities and Corrections (Colcord & Mann, pp. 99–104). What Richmond and her colleagues proposed was a school that was only loosely affiliated with a university and that would provide something more generalized than inservice training, but be less theoretical than university training. It would be like a medical school for those who were "doctoring social diseases" and would establish a "professional standard."

Richmond was able to bring all of the resources of the Charity Organization Society to her campaign to establish the school. Within a few months of her paper, the journal of the Charity Organization Society, *Charities Review,* carried an appeal for the program. One month after the article, in 1898, *The New York Times* announced a summer training program offered in New York for social workers. Six months later the program was hailed as a success by a national publication, the *American Review of Reviews.* (Ayres, pp. 205–206). The article also solicited funds, particularly from millionaire philanthropist John S. Kennedy. The appeal bore fruit and the summer program was continued for seven years (Meier, pp. 10–19).

In 1901, "The Committee on Philanthropic Education" of the Charity Organization of New York recommended that the summer school be extended to a one or two-year program. The two-year program began in 1903.

There was a strong and open involvement on the part of philanthropists in the formation of the school and the subsequent relationship to Columbia University. Philanthropists John S. Kennedy, Robert DeForest and J. P. Morgan were deeply involved. Kennedy was particularly active. He stipulated that the school maintain its independence or have no more than a very loose affiliation with Columbia. He also specified that a new Charity Organization Society Committee be responsible for the conduct of the school. The committee was to include the president of Columbia University, ". . . and other members satisfactory to Mr. Kennedy" (Ibid., p. 22). The aid they offered the school played an important role in the conservative bent that the New York School of Social Work was to take. It also would serve as a model for later schools of social work.

At about the same time that the New York School of Social Work was becoming a two-year program, the Boston School for Social Workers was founded. Although Mary Richmond and the New York Charity Organization Society seemed far away, Richmond and her agency were directly involved. She specified that the dean of such a school needed to be a college-educated man with a background in charity work. She successfully promoted a close associate and long-time friend, Jeffery Richardson Brackett, to be the initiator and administrator of the program (Lunt, p. 122).

Brackett was originally a sociology student at Johns Hopkins University. He became involved in charity work and was on the staff of the Baltimore Charity Organization Society, where he was closely associated with Mary Richmond. Brackett was part of the group that established the summer institute of philanthropy in New York in 1898 and was a lecturer there. In 1903 he published the first definitive book about social work education, *Supervision and Education in Charity* (Ibid., p. 121).

The Boston school was founded in October, 1904. Even before his appointment, Brackett was intimately involved with plans for affiliation. He had been recommended to Alice Higgins, general secretary of the Associated Charities of Boston, to assist in the development of the school by Mary Richmond. Brackett and Higgins corresponded extensively in planning the administration of the future school. Higgins referred to her committee as ". . . the group of conspirators" (Ibid., p. 148) and indicated that she had received assurances that Simmons College, then a school for women, would accept an affiliation in name only and give credit in its program for social work courses. In fact, President LeFavour of Simmons was part of the founding committee and was "willing to give a free hand." He was said by Higgins to ". . . realize the danger of the academic atmosphere as much as we ourselves do" (Ibid.).

Brackett was given an appointment in the department of social ethics at Harvard University prior to the actual opening of the social work school. He then worked with the committee to set up a nominal affiliation with Harvard University, as well as Simmons College, so that the school would be connected to both a prestigious men's school and a women's school. The relationship was consummated when the funds were donated to Harvard by philanthropist and Harvard graduate and supporter Joseph Lee specifically for the social work school. The administration of the school was left to the practitioners.

A financial issue finally put an end to the affiliation of the Boston School for Social Workers with Harvard. When it began to have financial difficulties the school requested assistance from Harvard. Harvard's contribution had always come from a special fund for the social work school. Additional monies would have had to come from the school's general fund. Harvard was unwilling to become involved in that way, and in the academic year of 1915–1916 withdrew from joint maintenance. The school continues to the present time as the Simmons College School of Social Work.

The problem of the use of university funds also caused problems at a social work school that developed in Chicago. The social work program began as part of the extension program pioneered by President Harper of the University of Chicago. As was the case for the Boston school the funds came from private sources. When the need for a larger budget developed another source of funds was sought. In 1906 the trustees of the Chicago Commons, a settlement house with close connections to Chicago's philanthropic community, voted to take full responsibility for the social work school. This suspended its relationship with the University of Chicago and the school became completely independent.

The trustees of the school were from philanthropic agencies and settlement houses. Chicago Commons, a settlement apparently more conservative than Hull House, was also involved in the program. In 1906, Graham Taylor of Chicago Commons was named president of the social work school. He responded to pressure for affiliation by the settlement people by pledging himself to such an arrangement when he began his duties. He claimed to have been planning such a merger for a decade and a half, but his efforts appeared to founder. Finally, a strong academically oriented faculty member, Sophonisba Breckenridge, when acting president while Taylor was on a two-month vacation, not only arranged affiliation with the University of Chicago, but gained the full support of the trustees. When he returned, Taylor resigned and Breckenridge became the dean of the new Graduate School of Social Service Administration of the University of Chicago (Ibid, pp. 130–139).

Thus all three of the original schools of social work kept themselves under the control of the Charity Organization and other practitioners early in their history. The effect of this was to have programs that were narrowly defined according to the needs of these agencies. What was taught involved technique for changing the psychology of the client, being his or her advocate in very specific non-controversial areas, and making judgments about the worthiness of clients and the well-being of children and other dependents. Social reform issues were either relegated to the background or judged to be unmanageable or inappropriate for the intervention of social work (Queen, p. 22).

In New York and Boston the character of the schools as outgrowths of philanthropic agencies continued through their early years. It was not until 1907–08 that teachers at the New York School were paid for their teaching responsibilities. The teachers were Charity Organization Society workers who volunteered their time or considered their involvement as part of their job responsibilities at the Society (Meier, p. 25).

The conflict over the leadership of these two schools further illustrates the direction they sought. The first dean of the New York School was Edward Devine, General Director of the New York Charity Organization Society. He continued to serve in both positions until 1907, when he resigned the deanship to function solely as administrator of the Charity Organization Society. At that time Samuel McCune Lindsey was appointed as dean. He was an academic, and social reform courses soon became the mainstay of the curriculum. His career as dean ended in 1912 when, by his own admission, his orientation conflicted with that of the trustees (Ibid., p. 40).

Edward Devine resumed the directorship in 1912 and held that position until 1917 when Porter Lee took the job and retained it until 1939. He also was from the Charity Organization Society and was strongly committed to their position. When Devine returned to the deanship

> The period in which emphasis had been placed upon economic history, economic theory, and socialistic experimentation was brought to a close. Social idealism gave way to "practicality" and to emphasis upon method and technique in social work (Ibid., p. 42).

A somewhat similar conflict over the deanship developed in the Boston School for Social Workers. Jeffery Brackett, unlike Devine, retained the deanship for an uninterrupted sixteen years. He retired in June, 1920. Although he frequently voiced approval of the academic approach in his writing, the curriculum in his school emphasized the practical approach (see, for example, Brackett, pp. 172–178). He also had a close working relationship with the Boston elite which included the prominent philanthropists of the time.

Brackett's successor, Stuart A. Queen, was different from Brackett. He was an academic and committed to dealing with social issues. He occupied the deanship for only two years. A history of Simmons College described his problem:

> Dr. Queen had been called upon to fill a position and meet a situation most difficult for a non-Bostonian. . . . For many years the management of local charitable organizations had been chiefly in the hands of a circle of philanthropic workers recruited largely from Boston's conservative aristocracy. Dr. Brackett had understood and cooperated with this group, for socially he was one of them, and, moreover, he was possessed of charm and tact. A newcomer from the outside doubtless could see where improvement might be made in some of the interlocking societies, but abrupt changes suggested by one who did not, indeed could not, absorb all of the subtleties of old Boston would meet with a cold response (Mark, p. 124).

Thus the original three schools of social work were able to remain separate from the academic world, at least temporarily. Other new schools of social work, founded between 1904 and 1916, were also independent and associated more with the Charity Organization Society than with any university (Hagarty, p. 52).

In addition to the Charity Organization people, there was a vocal group of people in social work who supported university affiliation. They were unsuccessful in their efforts, however, until pressures from outside the profession forced some accommodation with universities. By 1919 a change had apparently occurred. An Association of Schools of Social Work was formed with seventeen charter members. Nine of these members had strong university affiliation while eight were independent. The trend continued, and in 1931 the Association reported that twenty-one of its thirty members had full university affiliation. Furthermore, at that time the Association refused to accept any new independent members. By 1939 all association members were required to be affiliated with a university. (Hollis & Taylor, p. 29). The opposition to independent schools of social work from within and outside the profession eventually led to a gradual affiliation with universities.

The Pro-University Faction and Eventual Reconciliation of Social Work Education with Universities

The pro-university people had always been a part of the field, although not the strongest or most numerous group. As early as 1893 Homer Folks promoted the idea of the superiority of university-trained social workers (Folks, 1894, pp. 21–25). Another early social science scholar who promoted the close affiliation between universities and schools of social work was Charles Tufts. He felt a need for contact between social work and social sciences to promote growth in knowledge. The growing isolation of social work and its obsession with technique would, in his opinion, cause the profession to become rigid and stereotyped.

Edith Abbott, a leader at the Chicago school, decried the resistance to university affiliation (Abbott, 1942, pp. 1–19). She echoed Felix Frankfurter, one of the non-social workers, who also urged the profession to become "learned." Frankfurter suggested that:

> the university is the workshop of our democracy. . . . [It] should be the laboratory of this great new mass of scientific and social facts and the coordinator of these facts for legislation, for administration, courts, for public opinion. . . . Our task is to unify and correct the partial fact of the

all too scattered social sciences. . . . These schools [of social work] need the university. But the university needs the schools for social work . . . [to provide] the experience and the experimentation which. . . . [they] should produce. [The learned professions], necessarily specializations of one common endeavor, should be part of a single intellectual endeavor (Frankfurter, pp. 595–596).

Many of social work's critics were not as kind as Frankfurter. The price that social work paid for having separate schools was a lack of legitimation. University people turned the tables on the social workers and opposed the inclusion of social work material in their curricula. Content in social work was not seen as worthy of study and the practitioners were regarded with disdain (Walker, p. 160).

By far the most significant critic of social work education and the profession of social work was Abraham Flexner, a distinguished sociologist. He had been invited to address the 1915 Conference of Charities and Corrections. His topic was "Is Social Work a Profession?" (Flexner, pp. 576–590). He said that, in his mind, social work could not consider itself a learned profession in the sense that law and medicine were learned professions. The reason for this was that the field had no distinguishable knowledge base and no skills specific to itself that delineated it from other callings. These factors were necessary to have professional status. After the address a clamor arose in support of university affiliation, and continued until most of the schools had established a university connection.

An additional pressure for affiliation was the fact that universities, particularly the newer schools, began to set up their own schools of social work. These universities competed for students with the independent schools. The prestige of the university attracted many of the new people. Thus, after 1915, there was a gradual shift across the field toward university affiliation. The exception was the New York School. Here the commitment to independence was so strong that it was not until 1940 that the school of social work became an integral part of Columbia University.

In addition to pressure for university status, Flexner had another effect on the field. It responded to his paper with a vigorous effort to codify and institutionalize casework as a specialized knowledge base and a practice method unique to social work. In 1917 Richmond published *Social Diagnosis,* a book that became the seminal work in casework for many years. It delineated a special field of practice for social work (Richmond, 1917).

The emphasis on skills in casework and the narrow approach that focused upon the client and "retail" reform allowed for a return to the university without any danger of overconcern with ideological issues. Like the medical schools that Richmond tried to emulate, the schools of social work would become graduate schools. There would be a separation between the academics and the undergraduate programs. Furthermore, with the establishment of a unique field of knowledge, i.e, casework, the curriculum would be limited to this area.

A difficulty which had to be faced was the fact that students entering the schools would more than likely be college graduates. They would have exposure to idealistic and social reform perspectives. The resolution of this problem was possible because social work, early in its history, identified the characteristics of the "ideal" social worker. In many ways this ideal mitigated against social reformers. Admission requirements to the new graduate schools had to be developed to prevent entry of the students whose perspective violated this ideal or who could not be socialized to accept a more narrow perspective.

Chapter 5

Defining the Ideal Social Worker

With the introduction of graduate schools of social work a standard for admissions needed to be formulated. The graduate nature of the schools provided for the control of social work education by practitioners as well as distance between the professional schools and university undergraduate education. The problem that was created, however, was that new students would, for the most part, be college graduates. As such they would have been exposed to and potentially knowledgeable in the very ideologies that had been avoided by the separate status of the schools and the movement away from social science.

The schools of social work needed to develop careful standards. From the beginning of the profession there had been definitions of what would constitute the ideal social worker. Heavy emphasis was placed on attributes of personality. These conceptions had to be operationalized as entrance requirements and substituted for the usual academic prerequisites for admission to the social work programs.

The definition of the ideal social worker that was to be applied to applicants to schools of social work came from the Charity Organization Society. It was their conception that took hold because they had spearheaded the formation of the schools and raised the funds that made them a reality. The views of the settlement house people were different and constituted the opposition to the direction taken by the early schools.

The leaders of the settlement houses favored and advocated a strong liberal education for the potential social worker. They felt that this was the best preparation for professional work. They also treasured the diversity of their clients and saw their role as a sharing of cultures with others. This acceptance of diversity also applied to students of social work and neophyte workers. The settlement people did not specify personal characteristics in their workers with the care that characterized the Charity Organization Society.

The Charity Organization Society saw the dimensions of personality as the major factor in the determination of the ideal social worker. It included an anti-intellectual dimension that permitted the denigration of liberal education and an understanding of ideology as desirable attributes for social workers. The basic philosophy of the Charity Organization Society was one that prevailed as the image of the ideal social worker. It became the defined objective of social work education, i.e., the final product that the applicant or new worker was to become after his education.

The Philosophical Roots of the Charity Organization Society's Definition of the Ideal Social Worker

The keystone of this philosophy about human nature was the Protestant ethic, especially the concept of original sin. People were generally viewed as deficient in their natural state. Lust, emotion, laziness and faulty socialization frequently caused problems. These difficulties needed to be overcome; people needed to change. Such change could be brought about through proper socialization and the guidance and influence of a person whose success proved that he had taken the proper path.

This view of human nature was a consistent theme in the Charity Organization writings about the clientele of the agency, the programs, and the process of casework. It also applied to their views of the ideal social worker and the product that would be yielded by a social work education. In many ways expectations and judgments about students, staff and administrators were parallel to those made about clients.

Individualism and the work ethic were other cornerstones of this philosophy. Problems could be solved by an individual. A helper could be of assistance by addressing himself to the individual as opposed to changing the environment of the client.

Inability to solve one's problems was viewed as the direct result of not working hard enough, choosing the wrong path or going about one's tasks in an incorrect manner. In other words, a person's failure was proof that he or she had done the wrong thing.

Education was of value only if it served to improve the chances of a person's financial or personal success. Knowledge was specific to a student's need to grasp reality in order to solve his or her problems. Theory was defined as a more global understanding of the world and was considered much less important than knowledge. Fact was absolute and God-given. Its discovery required clearness of thought and common sense. Theory was from a different realm, unrelated to the real world. It was relegated to an avocation of the well-to-do. The focus of the social worker could not be in that area, and facility in dealing with theory was not only viewed as extraneous to social work but detrimental to reaching the status of the ideal (Mills, pp. 525–552).

Work was also God given. A person's calling had been divinely predetermined and success required clear thinking and the motivation to apply oneself (Weber, pp. 35–46). The problems that clients brought to the agency were, therefore, *prima facie* evidence of the failure of their methods of handling reality and the paucity of their motivation. Their need was to be set straight, to be rehabilitated, so that their behavior would ultimately result in success. The paragon they would need to imitate would be the ideal social worker.

Such a model had to be free of the unrealistic thinking that characterized the client. They could not demonstrate personal inadequacy, deviancy or other attributes of failure. In addition, the social worker needed to recognize his or her client's weaknesses and not exacerbate them. If the social worker followed his or her emotional inclinations he or she would be inclined to make grave errors. The root causes of the client's difficulties might be overlooked and sympathy for the client might lead to encouragement of the very behavior in need of correction.

Instead of simply following the natural desire to respond to the client's perceived needs, the trained social worker would see beyond the need for material assistance. The true needs had to be assessed in a scientific and unemotional way, the unworthy ones identified and sent on their way. Material assistance was to be given to meet only the most minimal and immediate needs so as not to encourage pauperism. Casework, the process of rehabilitation of personal deficiencies, would effect a permanent cure for problems.

There existed, therefore, in the neophyte social worker, inclinations that required change. These included sympathy for the client, a desire to provide material assistance and an unwillingness and/or inability to identify and attack the underlying, less evident causes of his or her client's problem. Furthermore, some people exhibited characteristics of a personal nature that were not unlike their clients' attributes. These people could be social workers only if they submitted to a change process which would bring their behavior into line with the expectations of the existing Charity Organization Society leadership. The process of social work education was designed to create such change.

The philosophical roots of the Charity Organization Society became an integral part of the education program of the new schools of social work because it was that agency's leadership that raised the funds to initiate the programs. This philosophy, taken from the Protestant ethic, emphasized the need to change the student based on the assumption that he or she was initially deficient. Thus education was designed to become a process to implement such a change.

Individualism played a strong role in the process of change. It promoted the notion that the difficulties of the student, worker or client could be ameliorated through individual problem-solving of a psychological nature. Involvement in global social issues became, therefore, unnecessary since the person could better his or her life and, more importantly, the client's life through this therapeutic process aimed at the individual.

The social worker, because he or she was to be an example for the client, needed to be a paragon, as noted above, of the virtues expected in the client. These dimensions of character or the projected ability to produce them became admission requirements to the profession and later to the schools. The focus denigrated the importance of a liberal education as a prerequisite for professional accomplishment and followed a general anti-intellectual bent that was also part of this orientation.

Early Charity Organization Society Views of the Ideal Social Worker

This philosophical viewpoint about social work education and students was first expressed as the agencies developed in-service training programs. Agencies were the only major training facilities before formal schools of social work were developed. In 1892 Zilpha Smith codified some of the principles of training (pp. 445–449). The new worker is perceived as naive and overly sympathetic. The educational process involved the student's loss of faith in simply giving assistance. What the social worker needed was to be convinced of the power of his or her personal influence. His or her services would uplift clients even after the crisis that brought them to the agency. The client would have access to the friendly visitor for as long as "uplifting" was necessary. Both client and worker were seen to be in need of personality change. The worker needed to be socialized to view the client as initially personally deficient and the client also needed to share this view, or at least claim to. He or she also needed to emulate the "friendly visitor" to correct personal behavior.[1]

Other expectations of new or potential social workers were specified

---

1. Zilpha Smith became a lecturer during a summer session at the New York School of Social Work and then the first major faculty member under Dean Jeffery Brackett at the Boston School for Social Workers. She played a major role in that school for the rest of her life.

by Anna Dawes. Her major interest was the recruitment of potential administrators for agencies in small communities. She specified that men would be preferable to women because they had more influence in the community. However, the salary was so low that it would be difficult to hire anyone who had more than a public school education (eighth grade) (Dawes, pp. 14–20).

An exception to the rule that low pay would discourage college graduates was the idealist who would be driven by "the missionary impulse." However, she rejected such a man because he "has his head full of science, but his opportunities for the practice of the art have been too meager for valuable results" (Ibid., p. 17). Thus education rather than preparation for charity work rendered the person unable to perform. Dawes suggested that it would be better for such a person to confine himself to settlement work.

Mary Richmond presented a much more detailed description of the potential worker. She first addressed herself to intelligence. This was defined as the ability to perform well in the world as measured by success in life. She specified that before becoming a charity worker, a person should have enjoyed success in another practical field such as business or teaching (Colcord & Mann p. 87). Charity work was to be a second profession.

Richmond preferred a person with a limited education. She specified that the individual should have "a good general education" but not be "specialized," i.e., academic. Also, like Dawes, she implied that certain aspects of education tended to interfere with the perception of the real world and rendered a person incapable of performing charity work. A good potential worker

> must have the faculty of taking hold of things by the right handle, a faculty closely allied with a good general education, and yet often divorced from it. In fact, a highly specialized education, one which had withheld a man for some years from his fellows and has prevented him from seeing much of life at first hand, would be likely to unfit him for effective charitable service (Ibid).

Thus Richmond perceived education as detrimental to personal functioning by preventing the individual from relating to other people. She specified that the candidate should have a good sense of humor, be imaginative, courageous, and sympathetic. His orientation needed to conform with existing norms and he had to have a strong orientation toward adjusting to the milieu rather than changing it. He had to be either narrowly political or apolitical. The political arena was seen as corrupt and corrupting. The avoidance of political values was a key attribute of Richmond's ideal social worker (Ibid).

The heavy emphasis on personal attributes led to heavy subjectivity in judgments about social workers in charity work and related fields. The range of acceptable candidates was narrowed down to those who supported these values. Any deviance, personal or physical, could be considered a basis for disqualification from the profession (Baldwin, pp. 393–394). The anti-educational, anti-intellectual position taken by Mary Richmond was pervasive throughout the Charity Organization Society literature. This orientation initially was reflected in the school programs.[2]

This view was not universal in the profession. Those social workers, the settlement workers and their aides, who favored social reform and direct personal involvement with their clients had a much more positive view of liberal education for the social worker.

To Jane Addams the client was not an emotional cripple in need of rehabilitation, but an individual deprived of opportunity. Given the chance, such an individual can eagerly take advantage of available resources. There is a need to provide resources, not to convince the client to change his or her ways (Addams, 1911, p. 371).

Most importantly, there is an inherent acceptance of diversity. Cultural differences are looked upon as a treasure. Familiarity with this diversity was a reward that accrued to those willing to become involved with people who were different. This acceptance of diversity applied to the notion of the ideal social worker. Specific delineations of desireable personality traits so common in the Charity Organization Society literature are not at all stressed in the settlement house literature. Instead, the focus is on people with intellectual resources who are willing to share. They needed the commitment to live and work with their clients. The social worker was not a role model but a friend and trusted adviser. In such a position there certainly was no need to concern one with being too much like the client. Erasing the differences between

---

2. Even those who were well educated themselves eschewed education for workers as a general principle. One such person even equated education with a lack of concern for people who have problems: "I should like to say something in regard to the parable of the Good Samaritan, especially with regard to the priest and the Levite who went by on the other side. Though it is not found exactly so in the New Testament, you will perhaps permit me, for my purpose, to call . . . the Levite and the university student . . . because I believe that (they) . . . are going by on the other side . . . there is a good deal of studying for the purpose of making books and speeches that does not reach the heart of the man who is in trouble." (Ayres, p. 451.)

people was part of the goal of the settlement houses (Addams, 1893, pp. 1–26). Just as there was an acceptable diversity of clients, there was also an accepted diversity of people who could become valuable social workers.

Addams recognized the elitist nature of certain kinds of education that separated the student from the "people." This did not render the scholar unfit for social work. Such a person could reeducate himself or herself so that communication could be reestablished. By such a process, a person alienated from others by his or her culture would be fulfilled by being brought into contact with them and by being useful to them.

The enhancement of communication was not only of personal benefit to client and worker, but it also made it possible to present culture to people in a meaningful way. Addams was painfully aware of the fact that class and educational differences interfered with her work. This was of particular importance in her political work, where she tried to organize voting blocks to elect reform candidates who would oppose city bosses. She often failed, and blamed her difficulties on her inability to understand and work within the context of her client's culture. She implored that cultural sophistication be included in social work education. In this area she respected the city bosses' ability to function within the value orientation of the client (Addams, 1898, p. 879–883).

Addams illustrates the difficulties of cultural differences between client and worker by relating a terrible blunder made by Hull House Workers. Upon the death of a foundling, workers requested that the county provide for the burial. The neighbors became outraged and took up a collection for the funeral.

> It is doubtful whether Hull House has ever done anything which injured it so deeply in the minds of some of its neighbors. We were only forgiven by the most indulgent on the ground that we were spinsters and could not know a mother's heart. No one born and reared in the community could possibly have made a mistake like that. No one who had studied the ethical standard could have bungled so completely (ibid., pp. 880–888).

There is in the above quotation a respect for the client's culture and the need for the worker to adjust his or her attitudes. This is in sharp contrast to the Charity Organization Society's attitude which is judgemental about clients' values.

There were many other voices in opposition to the anti-intellectual approach. Most gave some of the same reasons that Addams did for the value of a liberal education. There were additional reasons, however, that spoke to the need for well-educated people to assume obligations for the professionalization of social work (Folks, 1894, pp. 21–30).

In summary, the settlement people supported a liberal education as a prerequisite to social work practice. They felt it enhanced the life of the person and enabled him to share the benefits with his or her clients. This rewarded the worker by giving meaning to his or her life and enabling him or her to have access to the wisdom and beauty of the client's culture. In addition, this sharing of culture acted to erase differences between people by minimizing class and status differences between client and worker. This allowed for and even glorified diversity in both clients and workers. Social work was to create a multicultural pluralistic society where people would work together for the common good without regard to status and class. Therefore, the heavy emphasis on personality traits was far less important for the settlement people than it was for the Charity Organization Society workers.

There was some commonality of opinion between the two groups in regard for the need for change. The Charity Organization Society stressed change in personality so that the worker's behavior and personality were consistent with his values. The settlement people saw change in cultural sophistication and in the ability of the social worker to communicate it to the client. Both groups, therefore, supported the idea of graduate schools. The settlement people hoped eventually to influence schools to adopt a curriculum more in keeping with their values, but in the meantime acquiesced to the Charity Organization perspective. Their strongest influence was felt in Chicago, but their position was not considered in other schools for a long time to come.

Operationalizing the Ideal

Once the schools were established, the importance of personality and life experience over academic and intellectual qualifications still remained unresolved. Controversy continued in the social work education literature. Admissions criteria and evaluations gave priority to personal factors in students and workers. Because of continued pressure for education and experience in students and professionals, lip service endorsement of academic requirements can be found throughout the literature. The inability to adhere to these standards was often the subject of long and involved defense of the schools' non-academic expectations of applicant students and graduates.

In 1921 the new professional schools had become so identified with the Charity Organization Society that the agency became the standard against which all practice was measured.

. . . complications also arise from the domination of certain types of social work . . . this is especially true of the charity organization society movement. . . . It is not surprising, therefore, that family case work should sometimes be used as synonymous with social work, and that there should be a tendency in some quarters to judge the standing of social workers by training and skill in this particular field . . . (Steiner, p. 4).

It was clear that the early schools were set up as training facilities to meet the needs of agencies rather than in accordance with the ideals of university teaching. The schools did not have significant academic requirements for admission. Instead, they used personality attributes that conformed to the standards of the Charity Organization Society.

This emphasis upon academic attainments as a basis for social work must not force unduly into the background the personal qualifications that should be possessed by those seeking training in this particular field. . . . [The social worker's] services to individuals and community may be vital and based upon expert knowledge, but they do not always stand out in such a clear-cut and definite manner as they are easily understood and readily acceptable. For this reason, technical knowledge alone is not sufficient. The social worker must be a salesman, a promoter, and organizer. His personality should be such as would command respect and win confidence (Meier, p. 29).

The personal qualities that were so central to admission to these programs were very difficult to measure. Instruments used for measurement were considered even by their proponents as inaccurate and dealt with criteria that were irrelevant to the profession (Ibid., p. 39). A lack of standardization allowed for subjectivity in the selection process, with accepted students reflecting the narrow value orientation of the evaluators. Even such factors as personal reference were rejected. The schools were willing to trust only the judgment of the faculty.

The success of the promulgation of this notion of the ideal social worker was reflected by demographic studies conducted during the 1920s. One early study, conducted by the Russell Sage Foundation, reflected the anti-academic stance of the Society. It was reported that only about 44 percent of the social workers in the study had a college education (Walker, p. 116).

An additional study done in Philadelphia in 1925 showed that of the 60.1 percent of the social workers who had a high school education or less, 42 percent did not finish high school and 6.2 percent had only a grammar school education (Deardorff, p. 117). Another study of 66 agencies in Ohio showed that 23 had workers with only a grammar school education and 25 had workers with only a high school education. Only four agencies were staffed exclusively by people with a college education. In almost all instances agencies preferred a college education but did not require it.

Two-thirds of the social workers who took part in a Russell Sage Foundation study in 1922 were found to have had experience in other fields. However, these represented a broad spectrum of occupations with little common experience. Thirty percent of the population had been teachers. Twenty-one percent came from "business." Less than 10 percent came from each of the professions of nursing, ministry, journalism, and law. The study sampled 1007 women and 221 men (Walker p. 118). What this meant was that they were unwilling or unable to remain in their initially-chosen occupation. While this may be seen as an undesirable characteristic, it was in keeping with Mary Richmond's call for recruiting social workers from outside professions.

Walker gives a composite picture of the social worker of the 1920s. The character of the worker is somewhat at variance with the ideal, but can be seen as an outgrowth of the loose criteria being applied:

> Usually, the professional social worker is a woman who has had between 4 and 5 years experience in the field and is doing case work. She is working in a city of over 300,000 population and is receiving a salary of less than $800.00. She has had experience in some other field before entering social work but has not completed college nor a course in a school of social work. The chances are 3 to 1 that she will not rise to an executive position, 40 to 1 that her salary will never be over $3,000 annually, and almost 3 to 1 that she will not remain in the field for more than five years after entering it (Ibid., p. 123).

The field of social work received little respect from the community at large and from other professions. The above composite hardly suggested high status. Within the profession there was little communication between workers in different areas of specialization. Workers were preoccupied with specific technique in their narrow areas. To Walker this seemed to be a defense against a pervasive inarticulateness that existed in the profession. She suggests: "The finite mind falls back for comfort upon the actual situation which he knows: so the social worker appears to be an individualist" (Ibid., p. 134).

The profession was sorely in need of legitimization. One faction of social work, psychiatric social work, seemed to have an answer to this problem. It identified itself with psychiatry and the mental health movement. This profession had prestige and its new theoretical foundation, psychoanalysis, fitted the Charity Organization Society's concepts of the ideal social worker and the social work relationship like a glove. The assumption of client deficiencies, intrapsychic problem solving, the need for a psychologically healthy therapist and the almost mystical relationship between the mentor and the unfortunate client had direct parallels in early casework thinking. By the middle of the 1930s this psychiatric orientation became pervasive and left its imprint on the developing notion of the ideal social worker. It also justified the admissions criteria of the schools of social work and social work agencies who had the aura and jargon of a high-status medical specialty.

The Acceptance of the Psychiatric Knowledge Base and Its Effect upon Entry Requirements into the Profession and Professional Schools

From the beginning of the twentieth century, intrapsychic functioning was of interest to the social worker. This was particularly true of those who urged that the field concern itself mainly or exclusively with problem solving through personal adjustment rather than environmental manipulation. Educational content developed around this subject.

The movement toward this psychiatric knowledge base had enormous impact on the perceived qualifications of new workers and students. Psychiatry considered the concepts of "transference" and "counter transference" from psychoanalysis basic to the practice of psychotherapy. Transference involved infantile and inappropriate reactions of the patient toward the therapist. Certain contingencies in therapy and unresolved psychic conflict and/or neurosis in the therapist caused him or her to have a transference reaction called countertransference. This resulted in inappropriate and infantile emotions directed from the analyst to the patient. This was seen as having a seriously negative impact upon the therapeutic relationship and the outcome of therapy. The therapist had to control his or her feelings and resolve any neurotic problems that he or she had. The insight required for this came out of having a basically normal personality and, in certain instances where normality could not be demonstrated, treatment for the therapist.

Psychological health, therefore, was a prerequisite for the therapist. As social workers became predominantly therapists, the same criteria for emotional stability were applied. This stability very often implied compliance to rules, acceptance of the status quo in society and a calm non-assertive demeanor that often mitigated against social activism and people inclined in that direction. In addition, psychiatric diagnosis tended to be vague and broad enough so that it could be applied to a

large variety of people. Thus, many individuals with behavior unac-
ceptable to those in authority could be labeled through the use of this
diagnostic material.

An additional by-product of the psychiatric orientation was an application of principles of didactic psychoanalysis, the emotional re-
education of the student psychotherapist through a quasi-therapeutic
relationship with teachers and field supervisors in the social work field.
Where this was practiced, students submitted to searching and inti-
mate revelations about personal functioning, ostensibly related to relationships with clients, but often involving a broader analysis about the
student's functioning. Obviously this narrowed the field of students to
those wishing to submit to this kind of scrutiny.

The relationship in emotional education *qua* psychiatric treatment
was based upon transference. Thus the student as worker was viewed
as and encouraged toward an infantile, dependent, highly subordinate
relationship with his or her teachers and supervisors.

This psychiatric nature of social work education was exemplified by
what was known as the case method of instruction. This became the
foundation of the educational process. It involved process recording, a
close paragraph-by-paragraph examination of case material. Students
were asked to analyze the material for hidden meaning, visualize the
situation and comment about the decisions made. While at first it was
used to instruct workers in interview techniques and dealt with both
social and personal situations, the technique lent itself to the acceptance of concepts such as the hidden psychopathology of the student
and counter-transference reactions during the interview.

The psychiatric orientation further narrowed the range of acceptable
students for the field. The student needed to present himself or herself
as psychologically normal. He or she had to be willing to engage in a
process of learning that treated the student as if he or she was a child.
It is unlikely that an assertive social reform oriented student would
acquiesce willingly to such a relationship.

Finally this psychiatric evaluation had a chilling effect on the acceptance and success of students and workers who had indeed experienced
crises during their lives such as the death or suicide of a parent, incest
or other sexual or physical abuse, involvement in antisocial behavior by
themselves or even by members of their immediate families, or any
other behavior or event that could be viewed as psychopathogenic.
This was particularly true if these events were public. Often poverty or
involvement with agencies as clients could be detrimental to the later
admission of a person as a worker or student. Since the genesis of
behavior of all kinds was viewed as intrapsychic, environmental expla-

nations for the behavior was completely ignored. The functionalists were particularly rigid in adhering to this position and were a good example of how it was used to exclude people from the profession.

Assuring the Adjustment of Potential Social Workers

As we have seen, the functionalist school of social work practice was the most conservative and the most identified with service through individual therapy. Functionalists, therefore, presented the logical extreme of the psychiatric model. As described in Chapter Three, they acted to shift the profession away from concern with environmental issues.

In dealing with the issue of potential students and workers, they promoted exclusionary, arbitrary and subjective criteria. Virginia Robinson suggested that beyond knowledge, personality factors, although vague, were the key to performance in casework (Robinson, 1930, p. 168). These important traits seemed to have a mystical quality. A person with a pleasant personality may "lack the traits while a shy inhibited person . . . may develop more sensitive understanding. . . ." Both are seen in need of quasi-therapeutic education. The essential feature of applying these criteria is that there is the potential for creating arbitrary decision-making about students' and workers' performance and suitability for the profession.

Robinson sees the ability to perform in an emotionally stable way as a prerequisite to entry into schools and professions. Therefore the student who applied for such a program and was found to be emotionally wanting would not have the opportunity to resolve his problems in school:

> The first responsibility of the training schools upon whom the burden of this task falls is the selection of students who are capable of the development we seek. This is to measure potentiality, not actual presentability or performance, in applicants, for no student fresh from college has sufficient experience in relationships or enough understanding in differences in people, their backgrounds and behavior, to be able to meet the clients that come to the application desk of a social agency intelligently and helpfully. . . .(Ibid., pp. 171–172).

The judgments as to the suitability of the students are to be made through personal interviews. Robinson expresses doubts about psychological testing. She concludes that personal contact will "sound out the applicant's attitudinal equipment." This would be the best means for students and teachers to "find out whether social work is really the field to which the applicant is fitted. . . . " The content of the interview was again nebulous and personal. ". . . everything in the applicant's present situation, interest, ambitions, relationships, are pertinent and revealing" (Ibid., p. 72).

Robinson is very candid about the fact that information as to where to draw the line of rejection is unavailable. This does not prevent her from carrying on anyway, suggesting that admission judgments be made not only after the completed interview but even during the interview itself. She states: "in such interviews certain students are being discouraged and eliminated constantly for reason of attitudes which do not show promise of development or change in casework experience" (Ibid.).

The New York School of Social Work people added an additional dimension. Not only would a student with apparent emotional problems be assumed to be a detriment to his or her clients, but also would risk his or her shaky emotional makeup by engaging in social work:

> Our experience has led to the conviction that some method of selecting students for social work in general, and in particular for psychiatric social work, should be adopted which will more consistently exclude those persons who are so unadjusted or so immature as to make the study of mental hygiene in a professional school a serious risk to them (Lee & Kenworthy, pp. 257–258).

The personal interview was the method used to find the so-called emotionally unstable applicant and eliminate him or her from consideration. Although the process was used in many places, it was again the functionalists who leaned most heavily toward interviewing the applicant and using written material to uncover hidden psychopathology.

The functionalists controlled the school of social work at the University of Pennsylvania. Their influence remained strong from the late 1930s through the early 1960s. It was at that school that admission was determined mainly through psychodiagnostic technique. All application materials were examined with psychiatric scrutiny, beginning with the initial inquiry. Information for the interview process, i.e., questions to be asked of the applicant, was gleaned from the pre-interview materials with particular emphasis on the hidden meaning of written statements (Bishop, pp. 21–22).

While the applicant was asked whether he or she could attend an interview, a negative answer was *prima facie* evidence of possible unacceptability:

Experienced social workers and applicants who know something of the school seem to accept the requirement of an interview as a matter of course, while members of the younger group often hesitate to commit themselves to such a definite and troublesome step. When the question on the application blank about interview is answered "No" or "Only if absolutely necessary" I take this up with the applicant when the application is acknowledged. . . .

Asking applicants to come to the school for an interview, some great distances and at considerable expense, requires real convictions to the value and usefulness of this applicant. . . . I have no doubt that some applicants are cut off by the requirement, but I feel sure that those who really want to come to the school and have a real conviction about wanting to get its training somehow manage to come for the interview. . . .

Some applicants are not asked to come for an interview, a decision to reject being made on the basis of the written portion of the application. . . . very rarely are applicants admitted without an interview. A few exceptions are made for applicants from great distances . . . not more than four or five students a year are admitted in this way (Ibid., pp. 19–20).

The concern about the mental state of applicants became pervasive by the 1940s. All manner of dreaded motives were attributed to neurotic applicants. Even liberals such as Bertha Reynolds and a representative of the progressive Chicago school, Charlotte Towle, expressed the need for eliminating them from the field. Those who were emotionally disturbed were said to seek out the profession in order to cure themselves and to act out needs for approval or domination (Reynolds, 1942, p. 66). The neurotic needs supposedly satisfied by becoming involved in the human service professions are cataloged by Towle:

The responsibilities [of these professions] give promise of meeting the needs of such persons to repress, deny and disguise their strong dependency impulses, their need to strive to identify with authority, their need for social approval. In a culture where learning is loved, the learner gets a sense of being loved through the acquisition of higher learning. Their need to repress, deny, react against—that is compensate their hostile impulses through humanitarian work—their need to ease guilt through demanding work or devotion to a cause may seem to bring satisfaction (Towle, 1954, p. 77).

In elaborating upon this concept, Towle specifically identifies social concern as a symptom of neurosis:

With reference to the idea that certain professions attract specific neurotic personalities, one is reminded of the impression afloat that many "compulsive types" seek the profession and notably social work. Dr. Alexander states: "The typical compulsive is usually a highly intellectual person who has learned to detach his emotions from his reason. He is inclined toward abstract thinking, believes often fanatically in abstract causes and principles and is apt to neglect the practical aspects of life. He is loyal to causes rather than to persons, is a theoretical lover of mankind but somewhat detached from immediate associates . . . the letter of the law dominates his sense" (Ibid).

The method for selecting non-neurotic applicants continued to be a problem. Through the 1960s interviews and questionnaires were given and interpreted by faculty who claimed expertise in psychodiagnosis. Studies were performed to justify the techniques used based upon testimonials and case records. Very little statistical evidence was presented to justify the techniques. One study that attempted to report relationships between personality and success in social work claimed to have calculated correlations but never included the statistical material in the report. Instead, a broad sweeping statement was made: "When the data thus obtained were evaluated some significant correlations were noted between certain personality patterns presented by interview subjects and degree of success or failure in social work training and later job performance" (Berengarten & Kerrigan, 1968, p. xv). Which variables were correlated and how significant their relationship was, was left to the imagination. Nonetheless, the study is used as a basis for setting up criteria for the selection of students.

The psychiatric theoretical foundation developed in the 1930s became pervasive in the field. It affected admission requirements and the curriculum in schools of social work. The curriculum issues will be covered in the following chapter. The admissions requirements were designed to select non-neurotic applicants for schools and social work positions. They were judgmental and of questionable validity. Nonetheless they justified already established notions of the ideal social worker and gave an aura of scientism and professionalism to social work. They were therefore retained and defended, some to the present day, in spite of their deficiencies.

Summary

This chapter has looked at the image of the "ideal social worker." Early in the history of social work the Charity Organization Society delineated the character of the ideal social worker. Their delineation reflected the Protestant ethnic philosophy that underpinned the practices of the agency. The kind of person described narrowed the range of people to be admitted to the profession. What was emphasized was an anti-intellectual position that guarded against concern with ideology. Social workers were to be practical people who did not necessarily need a liberal education. They also were encouraged to be apolitical and not too concerned with global social issues. Theirs was to be a practice of adjustment to the social milieu rather than an effort to make broad changes. Mostly importantly their behavior was to be free of deviancy in that their professional role was that of mentor. This organization was operationalized in the entrance requirements of the new schools of social work.

This position was opposed by the settlement workers. A liberal education was viewed as an edifying resource to be shared with clients. Such a use of the worker's education gave meaning to his or her life. The rewards for such sharing also included contact with the diverse cultures of immigrants who constituted the agency's clientele. This diversity was treasured not only in clients but also in social workers. Therefore, the settlement people did not specify a social work ideal based upon personality characteristics as did the workers in the Charity Organization Society.

Nonetheless, the settlement people shared the notion with the Charity Organization workers that professional education was a necessity for social work. Both groups saw the need to enhance the ability of the social worker to understand the client in a scientific way. The settlement people, therefore, supported the schools in spite of their philosophy, hoping to make changes through pressure on ongoing programs.

The ultimate aim of these criteria was to produce practitioners of limited scope. The field developed legitimation through an intense and pervasive relationship with psychiatry and the mental health movement. This provided an image of respectability growing out of the status of medicine and a jargon that suggested a deep scientific understanding of human behavior. Many of the premises of this perspective exactly paralleled the criteria of the social work ideal but used the language of psychodiagnosis which had the necessary mystical quality.

The field attempted to develop devices to ferret out neurotic applicants to schools of social work. The effect was to narrow the profession still further. Evaluations were done so as to favor those who saw their work as individual therapeutic helping rather than activism and reform. Other elements of the evaluation tended to be subjective and brought a great deal of extraneous material into the application process.

The psychiatric orientation spread throughout the field and was accepted by all schools of social work. It was in keeping with a movement begun in 1917 and continued to become the mainstream of the profession. The development is clearly illustrated in the growth of the curriculum, the subject of the next chapter.

Chapter 6

The Curriculum in Social Work Education

The curriculum of any professional school not only reflects the content seen as desirable for the future practitioner; it also shows the issues being fought out between different factions of the profession. We have considered the issues of the knowledge base of the profession and the movement of schools of social work out of the colleges and universities. Just as the knowledge base of social work and university affiliation of schools were deeply rooted in concern with power and control of the profession, so too are those same power and control issues a foundation of the social work curriculum battle.

As we already know, it was the Charity Organization Society that prevailed. At the point of the legitimation of the curriculum, about 1930, it was their ideas that were the keystone of course content. Modifications that occurred after that time were in response to criticisms of the existing curriculum. Changes, when they did occur, were gradual and their proponents were hard pressed to have their ideas implemented.

The issues raised by criticism of the content were resolved by a process of cooptation by the Charity Organization people. There was general agreement as to the value of the opposition's ideas and nominal acquiescence to incorporation of their notions into casework. The apparent acceptance of the new idea was followed either by its being disregarded or redefined so that it lost its substance. In either event the caseworkers continued their original practices without making any changes and yet appeared responsive to new ideas.

The process of cooptation and redefinition can be illustrated by the Charity Organization's treatment of social reform issues. Reform was divided into "wholesale" or global reform and "retail" reform, specific to an individual case situation. The wholesale method, which ad-

vocated substantive societal change, was rejected as too cumbersome
for practice. The caseworkers opted for the retail method which
neither threatened their supporters nor established practice. In doing
so they could not be accused of being totally unresponsive to social
reform.

The capacity to operate in such a duplicitous manner grew out of the
way in which casework was pictured by practitioners. Its boundaries
were vague and nebulous. Definitions of the process of the core of
casework rehabilitation were so general that they gave little or no
direction and the impression that content was almost entirely lacking.
Emphasis was laid on ancillary activities such as diagnosis or investigation in discussions explaining casework. Instead of abstractions about
what casework accomplished and how it did so, the literature resorted
to case illustrations and narratives which were intended to speak for
themselves or illustrate a point when interpreted. Criticisms of these
factors resulted in acknowledgement of theoretical shortcomings owing
to the newness of social work and the hope that later work would fill in
the gaps.

The new worker was confronted, therefore, with a task that was
supposed to be of the utmost difficulty but could not be explained.
Agencies responded to the situations by developing elaborate and
lengthy in-service training programs to equip workers to take on the
tasks. This was the earliest education in the field. It provided the
foundation for the later schools of social work's curriculum.

Schools of social work were proposed as an alternative to the agency-
specific in-service training before 1900. The schools were said to teach
casework as a general technique encompassing practice in many settings. In reality social casework instruction was dominated by Charity
Organization Society methods and taught by Charity Organization Society employees. In effect it was still in-service training.

This narrowness of instruction became an issue of trying to resolve
whether schools of social work would concern themselves with training
or education. Training involved emphasis on specific techniques and
skills. Education spoke to the teaching of broad principles and expertise which would be meaningful to a diverse group of practitioners. As
the issue matured it focused on whether the curriculum should be
specialized or generic, related to all manner of social work practice. It
was agreed that a diverse program incorporating both training and
education should be included in the social work curriculum. Beyond
that agreement, no substantive change occurred in the programs.

The focus shifted during the first quarter of the twentieth century to
the generic versus specific issue. There was general agreement that the

curriculum should be generic, i.e., there should be an overall type of casework practice that applies universally. The term "generic" was redefined and said to mean that there was a common element in all practice. That was what needed to be taught. The common element to which all casework addressed itself was psychopathology. Therefore casework in the Charity Organization Society mold took on a psychiatric psychoanalytic appearance. The universality of mental illness in social work cases, regardless of specialty, justified its teaching to the diversity of students in the field. Because psychiatry, in many ways, ideologically mirrored casework, little substantive change needed to occur in basic practice or in the curriculum of social work.

Training versus Education

American pedagogy has long struggled with the issue of whether to concern itself with the provision of liberal education in broad areas or to provide students with specific skills with which they can enter the job market. Professional education is, by definition, concerned with the preparation of students to become practitioners in various areas. It must concern itself with the teaching of professional skills. The debate often arises as to where the line should be drawn between the skill content and the theory content. In social work the matter was complicated by the fact that the issues of theory and practice were intertwined with the struggle between the schools and agencies for control of social work education and, by implication, the direction of the profession. Agency control translates into a preoccupation with client rehabilitation. University predominance, while not a guarantee of concern with social reform, provided a greater inclination in that direction.

The founders of social work education had no doubts about the direction they saw the process going. Anna Dawes entitled her original request for the schools "*Training* Schools For a New Profession" (italics mine) (Dawes, pp. 14–20). Mary Richmond's famous appeal was a call for a "Need for a *Training* School In Applied Philanthropy" (italics mine) (Colcord & Mann, p. 99). The initial summer program sponsored by the New York Charity Organization Society as the first school of Philanthropy was referred to as ". . . a summer *training* school in practical philanthropy" (italics mine) (Ayres, p. 205).

The distinction between training and education was carefully delineated by Tufts in his *Education and Training for Social Work:*

> Training suggests primarily the acquirement of a technique, it implies,
> in Professor Dewey's description, formation of habits with relatively

little regard for the meaning of what is done. Vines and trees are trained; animals are trained; soldiers and apprentices are trained. . . . education, on the other hand, when distinguished from training, suggests rather an emphasis upon the full meaning of situations and experiences with which we deal. It suggests wide acquaintance with all aspects, and sensitiveness to all elements of culture and life. It involves methods of observation and inquiry which are more or less rigidly exact according to the subject matter and the progress of science, but it emphasizes the consideration of wide ranges of relevant facts and values. It involves consideration of ends as well as means (Tufts, p. 91).

Social work requires, Tufts argued, creative and well-educated minds. It was a profession in its own right. What was needed was creativity for its tasks. This creativity was necessary across the board. Issue was taken with those who felt that such a broad education should be reserved for administrators. Such elitism would produce friction in the profession and denigrate direct practice. In the absence of creativity and education, the practitioner's job became deadening and routine and without the substance to deal with new conditions by inventing new methods. On the other hand, the administrator with only an education could, with justification, be accused of being outside of the real world of practice (Ibid., pp. 95–96). Tufts opted for a program of both training and education. Although he saw the possibility of short-term division of the profession along a hierarchy of educational levels, the need for sensitivity to the broader issues was required for all levels of practice and administration. The division was to be temporary.

Tufts recognized severe problems in the implementation of such a program. He felt that recruiting a sufficient number of people who would invest themselves in such an educational process would be difficult. This problem occurred because there were no rewards for the acquisition of an education. Agencies did not pay people who had education more than those who did not. Tufts therefore allowed for the reality that some practitioners should be trained to meet immediate professional needs. The brief and undemanding nature of this process might attract a greater number of students. Agencies might also be more willing to reward and even finance a process that responded to training needs as they defined them. This, it was felt, would set the stage for the introduction of a broader educational program as the profession matured (Ibid., pp. 98–101).

Unfortunately, by the early 1920s, rather than the maturity Tufts envisioned, many schools, including the New York School, Pennsylvania School, Bryn Mawr and Smith, had institutionalized courses that could still be criticized as in-service training programs (Falk, pp. 56–

57). The issue was a matter of deep concern among the liberal leadership of the profession.

Instructors in the schools were predominantly practitioners rather than teachers from a university. The emphasis upon such training and agency control led to a denigration of social work education in the eyes of the academic community. University faculty schools of social work were regarded as "normal schools," rather than "professional graduate schools" (Steiner, p. 42).

The outcry and debate around the issue of the training function that schools of social work had assumed was evident in the formation of the Association of Training Schools for Professional Social Work. This organization held its first meeting in 1919 with faculty representatives from the 15 graduate schools that had come into existence at that time. The name and form of the organization had been developed by a committee of five. This committee was appointed at an earlier informal meeting called by the agency-oriented dean of the New York School of Social Work, Porter Lee.

The conservative weighting of the association caused Edith Abbott of the University of Chicago to react in 1922. She saw the word "training" in the name of the organization as not merely semantic but significant in terms of how social work education was conducted. She proposed that the association be called the American Association of Schools of Social Work. At the association meeting of 1923 the change was finally voted upon and adopted. Nonetheless, subsequent documents continued to use the old name for some time. Abbott persisted:

> We have not only been asked, we have, in fact, scarcely been allowed to develop a solid and scientific curriculum in social welfare. Instead of that, we have been asked to provide "training courses" . . . (Abbott, 1931, p. 30).

Casework methodology, case conferences and field work, if not the exclusive curriculum, certainly had become its core. Field work amounted to a part-time apprenticeship in an agency for which the student was given credit. It involved intense supervision where the work was carefully scrutinized by an agency practitioner called a "field instructor." This person generally was available to the student and also scheduled regular weekly case conferences to review specific work being done by him or her.

Such a regimen was not unlike in-service training for a new worker. There were, however, two components that made the students' experience different from that of a new worker. There were a multiplicity of courses given that were outside of the core. These were a variety of courses that were included in the curriculum in response to pressure for broadening social work professional education. They varied over time and often from school to school depending upon the issue that was popular at that place and time. In the main, they had little or no impact upon the thrust of social work education particularly before 1930 (Steiner, pp. 41–51).

The second component that distinguished the school from an in-service training program was a course, taught at all schools, called "casework" or "casework methods or practice." This course was designed to teach the skills of the major method of practice. The field sought to deal with the subject that it defined as so complex that it did not lend itself to the ordinary methods of teaching or explanation. The techniques for dealing with complexity were called the case method. It was first used by Mary Richmond, as previously noted. The method, originally a research technique, was combined with certain perceptions of legal education to create a teaching technique unique to social work education (Colcord & Mann, pp. 309–319).

The case method was ideal for teaching casework as portrayed in the literature. Definitions were vague with little information to develop the helping process that was claimed to be the core of casework. The only specificity one found had to do with concrete aspects of the process such as collecting information or determining the need for a financial grant (Halbert, pp. 56–57).

When pressed for more specific definitions of practice, practitioners suggested that actual practice was an art rather than a science. By this they meant that practice did not lend itself to exact explanation. It was an extremely complex method, requiring intense training and long experience to understand (Smith, pp. 445–449).

The Case Method of Instruction in Social Work Education

The case method involved a careful description of an individual client's situation, including written records of interviews. This case situation was then used as an example of a concept. It thus did away with the need for conceptual structure or definition. Generalizations could similarly be drawn from specific cases in the absence of intellectual standards for knowledge.

Sheffield discusses four aspects of case situations that are illustrative of the use of these cases in the case method (Sheffield, pp. 790–80). "Content" is the actual objective observation in the case. "Scope" deals with the range of the persons affected and the time required for development of the distinctive aspects of the situation. "Pattern" refers to the way in which the aspects organize themselves, that is, how they are distinctive. Finally, "process" relates to the course of change in people and circumstances over a period of time. Content, scope, pattern, and process, when interpreted in detail, provided theoretical insight and knowledge in the casework technique, according to Sheffield. The format, to a greater or lesser degree, characterized the dimensions ordinarily analyzed in the case content orientation.

This case method was detailed and specific. For that reason it was claimed to be an inductive method of reasoning. Apparently, the preoccupation with detail and specificity led one author to the conclusion that the method was "the method of science that begins with the concrete fact instead of the general principle" (Steiner, 1921, p. 52). The argument is that observations are made and conclusions drawn from observations. In reality assumptions about human functioning and individual cases generally were made although not always acknowledged. Evidence supporting that assumption was then sought through various interviews and observations.

For example, the notion of financial assistance creating dependency was a basic assumption of the Charity Organization Society. This was called "pauperization." To demonstrate the pauperization of a client, cases were selected where observations supported the assumption. Where poor people were involved very often pauperization was suspected. Interviews and case records were then used to support the assumption that the family under question was pauperized. When brought into the classroom, cases could be used to demonstrate the various dimensions of pauperism for the students new to the field.

Tufts traced the origin of the method to legal education (pp. 183–192). In the legal profession, he argued, the student gains knowledge of the common law by analysis of decision rather than study of textbook theory. The method teaches the student to find the law as it appears in the primary source and gives the student an appreciation and training in analysis and processes of judicial reasoning (Ibid., p. 184).

Tufts points out an important difference between social work and the law. In law the student can refer to judicial decisions and legal decision making as overriding principles in his or her reasoning. The case method, therefore, simply is a means of deriving principles from primary sources. In this sense, then, it is inductive. In social work the subject matter is treatment and diagnosis. Vague ideas such as "pauperism" exist rather than judicial decisions. It is against these vague ideas that the student tests his or her conclusion. Thus, the method is not as sound in social work as it is in law.

Tufts recognized the deficiencies in available knowledge (Ibid.,

p. 192) and suggested that some of these deficiencies might be overcome by each student having a strong background in social science.
However, the lack of a firm knowledge base was evident and disquiet-
ing to Tufts.

The adoption of the case method had certain immediate effects upon
social work education. Case specificity diverted the field from broad
concerns. By rejecting statistics, the social worker could also reject
findings that did not support the profession or its agencies. The full
weight of statistical measures of the ineffectiveness of casework was
pushed into the background by this adoption of the case method. It
wasn't until the 1970s that the accumulated evidence became so over-
whelming that it could no longer be ignored (Fischer, 1973, pp. 5–22).

The heavy emphasis on the case method would lead one to believe
that there was an identified group of clinical skills that needed to be
transmitted to students. The argument for case method emphasized
treatment in the prevention and amelioration of personal difficulties
such as child neglect, alcoholism, and similar social problems that
beset the poor and other clients. In reality, actual case work practice in
the 1920s and beyond basically was mostly involved with relief giving
(Hellenbrand, p. 61). Therefore issues that concerned the workers
involved specific and narrow factors such as eligibility, discovery of
fraud, and prevention of different agencies giving assistance to the
same families. Theoretically, then, social work looked upon assistance
as secondary to intensive case work services for each client. In reality,
intensive case work services were not available. This troubled the
practitioners and the suggestion was made that the relief budget of
agencies should be sacrificed for the "services" that caseworkers should
provide (Lynde, pp. 135–144).

The substance of case method and case work training lagged behind
the so-called need for service. Even though lip service was given to
"client-worker relationship" and "leadership in treatment," none of the
syllabae of the 1920s contained any significant incorporation of psychological material. Much of the reported content of courses dealt more
with the behavior of the workers than of clients. Such areas as the
effect of the worker's attitudes, prejudices, professional relationships
with other agencies, and the possibility that the worker might promote
conflict by carrying out his or her duties, were preeminent in the
curriculum material (Hellenbrand, pp. 119–121).

Case records, such as they were, were hard to secure. Although a
few texts of case material were in preparation in the 1920s, by and large
teachers themselves were responsible for finding and editing case rec-

ords. Very often only a very few cases were available to students, creating the illusion that their content could be generalized. Worker activity then became stereotyped and unresponsive to the unique qualities of the individual situations (Steiner, p. 56).

Agencies explained their reluctance to share their records with the argument that it violated confidentiality. It was suggested that untold damage could be done by exposing this material. Students and teachers were said to need vast and deep knowledge before they could legitimately approach this case material:

> In social work, the situations are very different [then in other professions using the case method]. The cases deal with human beings and family relationships, and feelings are injured and individuals and families are often humiliated when publicity is given to their problems . . . because of this some cases cannot be used, and in others, only a limited publicity can be given to them. In accomplishing the latter purpose, many cases are not printed but are typewritten and placed in the hands of teachers of social case work with the understanding they should be used cautiously. . . . The case method of teaching is difficult and should not be used by anyone except those who have the background of training and knowledge to use it successfully. . . . those who are receiving training to handle these intricate and difficult problems should be permitted to see all the elements which enter into the solution of difficult unit situations (Hagarty, pp. 134, 139).

This material suggests hushed discussions in dark rooms about cases that reveal the secrets of life. The truth was that the substance of the records lacked content. While the confidentiality issue and the importance of the expertise of users were stressed, the reality seemed to involve the mystification of pedestrian practice. What was created was an illusion of substantive professional activity. What seemed to be a commitment to progressive ideas of education relating to "learning from life" and discussion rather than lecture methods of teaching often were simply justifications of teaching materials without substance and a theoretical framework (See Mathews, pp. 45–66).

Teachers faced an inability to conceptualize with any degree of integrity. In her autobiography, Bertha Reynolds stated[1]

---

1. Bertha Reynolds was a leader in the teaching of social casework during its early development at Smith College. She came to be known, not only as one of the most progressive thinkers of her time, but as a candid and insightful observer of the field and her own participation in it as she functioned in practice and teaching.

My educational theory went wrong, I now believe, for two reasons. First and obviously, my own theory of social casework was too undeveloped to lend itself to lecture presentation, and my strong belief in the discussion method of teaching was partly a defense against the paucity of my own equipment. . . .

Many students had come to Smith from middle and farther western states which exaggerated the educational prestige of the East. They had heard that Smith was tops and would expect a lot of them. They were prepared to fill notebooks and to sit up nights learning the contents. What did they find? Kid stuff! Exercises in observation, little plays to see how everyday people interviewed each other, illustrations from life, instead of from the big hospitals and from books (Reynolds, 1963, pp. 88–89).

Reynolds and others were not at all satisfied with this state of affairs. In spite of the fact that they participated in casework education, they pressed for the adoption of broad frames of reference. Even many of those thoroughly committed to the case method and casework did not deny the existence of environmental causality for people's problems. Rather, they suggested that alternatives should be tried to allow the client to cope with the hostile environment. In short, they did not deny the importance of the environment, rather they chose to ignore it (Robinson, 1930, pp. 25–29).

There had been earlier efforts to broaden the base of casework education even before its institutionalization in 1930. The most significant effort culminated in the Milford Conference in 1929. The conference developed an ambitious group of recommendations only to find that the term generic had been redefined in psychiatric terms, and in substance was merely Charity Organization Society casework. It was the social work method. In the sense that casework retained its narrow perspective, the Conference did not achieve its goals.

The first element of the Milford Curriculum was called the fundamental techniques of social work. These techniques were identified as social case work, community organization, group work, social research, and administration. This particular group of courses became what is now known as the "methods" component of the curriculum. Case workers were to do classroom work in case work and also study in other areas.

Adaptations from science and experience from other fields for the purposes of social case work was the second suggested area. The Milford Conference suggested such subjects as psychology, psychopathology, law, health and disease as part of this particular section. The content here, too, became closely supportive of a rehabilitative framework.

The third dimension of the curriculum was called the practice of social work. It included field work and field-specific course work. It provided the agencies an opportunity to teach material specific to their practices. It was a compromise allowing for specialization in a generic curriculum design.

The fourth division of the Milford Curriculum was called "orientation of the social worker." It had to do with analysis of case work itself. Both in the field and class this was to deal with elements of case work that were philosophical and interpretive. In the discussion of this dimension, it was noted that "there is no better place" to learn this material than in supervisory relationship in the field. The subject could be handled in the classroom "when resources permitted . . ." (Ibid., p. 81). Thus the philosophical orientation of the profession was also controlled by agencies, as in the early in-service curriculum. This emphasis on field teaching diluted discussion and retained strong practitioner bias.

The Milford Report, though often quoted, was limited in its impact. Its influence and acceptance varied from school to school (Levy, p. 50). The aspect of the conference that took root was the one that provided legitimation for the domination of the field by casework. While not intentional, the outcome of the Milford Conference acknowledged the central importance of casework. This, along with recommendations of psychiatric social workers to the conference, allowed for the preservation of classical casework as the foundation of social work practice.

Psychiatric Case Work and the Milford Conference

The most elite of the specialties was psychiatric social work. It developed an alliance with the field of psychiatry that gave it an aura of professional legitimacy. As early as 1919, Mary Jarrett suggested that all social case work was psychiatric in nature (Jarrett, pp. 587–593). In 1925 Dean Porter Lee and Mary Antoinette of the New York School presented a paper that also held the position that psychiatric information was intrinsic to all social work. Their paper, presented to the Milford Conference, was adopted as the standard of all social work education.

This psychiatric standard served the purpose of redefining the training versus education debate. The original argument had been about agency control of schools and educational processes. This was no longer seen as a relevant issue. The problem with agency control was that it created specialized training. By making the content relevant to all fields of practice, i.e., generic, this drawback could be eliminated. The agency control issue no longer needed to be addressed. All areas of practice, psychiatric social work, medical social work, family social work, corrections and charity work, would be viewed and taught from within a psychiatric framework. A generic curriculum with its roots in psychiatry provided strong identification with a high status profession. Social work could be taught in the same way that it had always been taught, with the addition of some psychiatric jargon.

Critics who concerned themselves with agency dominance were quieted by this apparently scholarly approach to be applied across the board. The Milford Report seemed to gain acceptance, allowing social work education to create the illusion of the existence of a broad knowledge base drawn from the medical practice of psychiatry. The pursuit of technique could no longer be considered narrow training, but simply the logical next step. In other words, now that social work had achieved a legitimate theoretical foundation, it had matured to professional status. A generic curriculum allowed it to concern itself strictly with methodology (Hellenbrand, p. 59). Broader issues were irrelevant, social reform beside the point. The psychiatric thread had become the woof and warp of social work education. Only Community Organization was seen as separate from this perspective.

Community Organization

Settlement community workers not involved in social action worked in agencies such as the YMCA, Boy Scouts, community centers, and in the general aspects of recreation and adult education. The methodology of these workers remained vague and more undefined than that of the social case worker. Furthermore, the way in which they went about practice, because of their orientation in "Christian Socialism," was basically non-confrontational. Eventually, rather than rallying people to causes related to social issues, they concerned themselves predominantly with building neighborhoods, enhancing communication, forming clubs and helping communities identify common interests (Ibid).

The Charity Organization Society sought to promote cooperation between agencies and therefore made better use of resources by preventing the duplication of services and exposing impostors who wrongfully, in their minds, acquired financial assistance. Their efforts between agencies also prevented such people from gaining assistance from more than one agency. In addition to this role, they took on the job of raising the necessary funds for the agency's functioning (Dunham, pp. 37–38).

These community organizers quickly became strongly identified as agency representatives in large fund-raising appeals that eventually became community chests. Their specialty was based on a relationship with the affluent. Because of that, they eventually controlled the purse strings of their social agencies. Since their constituents were the wealthy, they concerned themselves with being representatives of that population. It is no wonder, then, that they were not advocates of the poor, but rather the spokespersons of the rich. It was the friendly visitor, later known as the family caseworker, who was responsible for direct services to the poor. The community organizer did not develop a practice that related to the broader aspects of the problem faced by clients simply because it became irrelevant to his or her constituency. The poor client basically became invisible to the community worker (Ross, p. 4).

With almost all of the emphasis in social work education on generic practice, little or no pressure was put on community organization to give up its status as a *bona fide* specialty. Its lack of methodology and theory was never challenged. It simply continued to function in a non-confrontive manner. Not only did the settlement workers not challenge the preeminence of the community chest organizers, they joined them. Therefore the entire field took on the character of the role defined by the fund raisers. Functionally, this particular specialty provided a place for community-oriented social workers to practice without challenging existing societal structures. In 1918 community organization officially accepted its fund raising role when it organized into the American Association for Community Organization, which became known as the Community Chest and Councils of America. In 1956 this association was renamed United Community Funds and Councils of America (Dunham, p. 42).

The education of community organizers was a late development of the social work curriculum. Although there had been institutes given over the years such as one offered through the Ohio State University in 1923, it was not until 1932 that the first community organization grouping appeared in the minimum social work curriculum (Hollis & Taylor, p. 41). Only the potential for social action remained.

This potential was disturbing to some caseworkers. A most revealing perception of community organization is offered by a much quoted description of behavior *required* of community organization for it to be considered social work. The three requirements involved functioning within a democratic process, a helping rather than a "controlling relationship," and a process that helped people find "satisfying and fruitful social relationships . . . not to the attainment of specific preconceived products of relationships (Pray, p. 428)." It is not difficult to conclude that the final parameter is an oblique reference to activities that would lead to social reform. For community organization to be considered social work, according to Pray, it needed to avoid confrontation and class struggle.

It was not until the 1960s that community organization (as well as the rest of the field) became aware of an activist role in social change. For the formative years of the relationship of social work and social reform, the specialty of community organization can be dispatched as irrelevant to the issue. The resolution of the reform issue through cooptation in community organization was even more complete than it was in the main body of the profession that concerned itself with casework.

The cooptation indirectly led to the brief leadership of reformers during the Great Depression. By the 1930s social work appeared to be a profession that could deal with the range of social problems from individual problems to social reform. In reality those social workers who undertook professional education received little or no preparation in anything besides casework. The Great Depression created an enormous need for reformers rather than for professionally educated clinical social workers. Only those people whose experience came from the settlement houses were able to meet that need. Many did not receive their education in schools of social work. Those who did, found it irrelevant. Their expertise came from another area. We will now examine this period of history and the rise of the reformers temporarily to preeminence over the caseworkers in professional social work.

Chapter 7

The Golden Age of Social Work Activism: The New Deal

The trends and activities thus far discussed have shown a profession born in social change realigning itself away from its original objectives. These changes have been illustrated over and over again in the founding of schools of social work, the professionalization of social work practice, and the policies and curricula of newly developing schools as well as the profession. Social work in general, and the schools in particular, came under the control of casework practitioners.

Because of coalitions between caseworkers and wealthy philanthropists, the profession developed a stake in the maintenance of the existing power and status relationships. As such, social work had to be moved away from its posture of social reform. By the end of the 1920s the social reform element in social work education was either absent in the schools or difficult to recognize. This was true both of the curriculum and in the activities of the schools and their faculties.

In spite of this, social work education has never been able to escape the fact that, within its ranks, there existed the remnants of those committed to the earlier professional values of social change. This opposition to the abandonment of social reform was in evidence throughout the development of the schools. Although the mainstream of social work education came more and more under the control of the conservative elements, concessions and compromises kept the concept of involvement in change from totally disappearing. Those that were responsible for creating the changes in the profession needed to constantly acknowledge, at least verbally, the importance of the environment and justice in the practice of the profession. The movement away from reform required lip service to an ethic of reform, environmental manipulation and justification of the strategy of non-involvement in vital issues. While it was true that social work had set out upon a course of questionable worth to clients, it was also true to the remaining reformers that the course required navigational adjustments and redirection so that the profession could never obliterate what its direction, what its occasional destination, had been.

The Great Depression upset the balance that had been set. At the highest levels of government the battles that had been fought in the profession of social work became national issues. The poor were no longer a foreign group of parasitic aliens that could be held at arm's length and derided for their moral depravity. Poverty, unemployment, and suffering became widespread and therefore destigmatized. The financial inequities in our society grew in prominence, became clear to the general public, and seemed to demand rectification. Within this context inaction became unthinkable, reform a conservative strategy, and revolution a solution with a growing number of adherents, therefore becoming a genuine possiblity.

Social work could no longer maintain its posture of non-involvement in reform. The long-dormant, liberal, settlement house wing of the profession, concerned with social issues, sprang into prominence. In a very real sense, social workers of this ilk became the heart and blood of the New Deal. Their ideas provided life and sustenance to the various elements of the Roosevelt administration's social programs. It appeared that social work was providing substance for a new era of social progress. Social reform suddenly seemed to be the mainstream of the profession (Leiby, 1978, pp. 240–243).

Beyond the activism of the "New Deal social workers" a substantial group of professionals supported radical action. These were the socialists who separated from the so-called "professionals" who occupied administrative and supervisory positions during the implementation of the social programs. They organized themselves into the "rank and file" movement in social work (Ibid., p. 243), and concerned themselves with a broad range of issues including international issues, such as the rise of fascism and civil rights before these issues became evident to others. Their solutions to the Depression involved a redistribution of power and wealth early on. Throughout the 1930s they chided the professional leadership and often played a role in the encouragement of substantial reform (Fisher, 1936; Spano, 1980).

The conservative elements in the profession verbalized support for the changes that were taking place. Beyond that support, however, they continued to promote activities in the profession that would eventually return it to the casework cause that neglected reform issues. As usual, they justified and promoted psychotherapy in social work practice and the therapeutic modality in education. They often became embroiled in esoteric psychotherapeutic controversy. Most importantly, they retained control in two vital areas that eventually restored their leadership to the profession. First they controlled the private agencies and promoted the cult of professionalism associated with psychotherapy. Young workers concerned with status often gravitated toward this practice. The second area where control was not relinquished by the conservative professionals and, strangely enough, not challenged by the New Deal social workers, was in social work education. Here they maintained the course of study that continued to be heavily oriented toward casework and disregarded the New Dealers. These New Dealers attempted to persuade the school leadership of the importance of content that related to public welfare, but never managed to dislodge the caseworkers from their positions of power. Students and faculty continued to support and teach a curriculum that would pepare the new professionals for the high status positions in the private agencies where the methodology was clearly psychiatrically oriented casework. In the end it was this group that determined the shape of the profession as the heady reform period of the New Deal subsided.

The Depression and the Rededication of Liberal Social Work to Social Reform

By and large, the attitudes of the two presidents that led the United States during the 1930s directly paralleled the two major positions that the social work profession held during the same period of time. Herbert Hoover's position was not unlike that held by those who were part of the Charity Organization Society; while the position that eventually was assumed by Franklin Roosevelt closely paralleled the positions of those people who were associated with the settlement houses. In order to illuminate the times and get a perspective on the different positions, we will examine the backgrounds and philosophies of the two presidents that governed the country during the depression years.

Hoover and Roosevelt: Two Views of Social Welfare[1]

Herbert Hoover was the quintessence of Mary Richmond's ideal social work administrator. He was a self-made man of American mythology (with a lot of help from his uncle). The son of a Quaker blacksmith and agricultural salesman, Hoover was born in Iowa in 1874. When he was six his father died. At the age of 10 his mother could no longer support

---

1. The material about the two presidents draws heavily on Hofstadter, 1948, pp. 281–352.

him. Therefore, he went to live with an uncle in Oregon. This uncle was a successful real estate broker. He raised Hoover and eventually employed him as an office boy. Through his influence, the new Stanford University relaxed its entrance requirements and admitted Hoover. He was a popular student and graduated with a degree in mining and engineering.

Because of the economic depression at the time of his graduation, it was necessary for Hoover to work as a gold miner in Nevada City, California. This lasted only a few months until he was able to secure a job as an office assistant in a San Francisco engineering firm. Through this firm he quickly found and moved into a position directing gold mines in Australia at the age of 24. Before he was 40 the opportunities opened to him by this job made him a millionaire associated with a score of business concerns in far-flung areas of the world. By 1911 he had been involved in business enterprises in Australia, China, Japan, Transvaal, New Zealand, India, Rhodesia, Egypt, Burma, Malaya, Ceylon, Italy, Russia, Korea, Germany, France and England.

Because he was a Quaker and an internationalist, he opposed war and was of some value to the Wilson administration because of the objectivity that these affiliations gave him. The objectivity with his business prowess led President Wilson and his successors to appoint Hoover to various activities involving benevolent and philanthropic work throughout the world. This was of importance during World War I and after the war when he was active in the attainment of the preservation of peace. In this sense he became deeply involved in social service although he never identified himself as "social worker." His success in this area far outdistanced even his substantial business accomplishments.

This "social work" career began when Hoover was appointed to help thousands of American tourists return home when they were stranded in Europe by the outbreak of World War I. He then accepted chairmanship of the Commission of Relief in Belgium. In spite of obstruction from both sides—Germany and the Allies—his Commission was able to feed ten million people for four years. His efficiency was so great that his demonstrated administrative costs were ⅜ of one percent when the program ended. As a result of this, there was a final surplus of funds sufficient to aid in the reconstruction of Belgium after the war.

In 1917 Hoover became food administrator in the United States and gained fame for his ability to conduct a program of food supply and conservation. He also had spectacular success in the economic restoration of Europe when he distributed 20 million tons of food, restored communication, and directed shipping fleets, railroads, and coal mines.

In a time of havoc and hatred the name Hoover came to mean food for the starving and medicine for the sick. From the ranks of his co-workers a fanatic body of admirers gathered around him. In several European countries streets were named for him. After five years of war service without salary and without attention to his private affairs, his fortune had been somewhat scaled down, but he was rich in popularity (Hofstadter, 1948, p. 285).

It is hard to believe that this watchword of benevolence and human kindness became a president vilified for being responsible for the deepest economic depression in the history of the United States. It is even harder to understand how a person so deeply involved in success-ful philanthropic work could be so paralyzed in the face of hunger and desperation during his administration that he found himself turning the Army against hungry demonstrators in Washington.

The cause of the turnabout in Hoover's fortunes can be laid upon his rigid ideology. The performance of his administration was said to be:

. . . one protracted rite of Hara-Kari. No president, even Grover Cleveland, has ever been seduced by his conviction into blunter defiance of the majority opinion. On this score, Hoover can always be acquitted of the charge of revising his ideas to cater to mass sentiment (Ibid., p. 286).

This fatal ideology was identical to the mainstream of social work philosophy as characterized by the Charity Organization Society. It promoted individualism and progress. The benevolence and steward-ship of wealth of the progressive business community was worshipped as the vehicle through which temporary setbacks in the economy could and would be offset. Assistance would result from volunteerism rather than from mandatory taxation. Thus, sacred capitalism would be pre-served and the poor would be set upon a course of self-help. There would be a minimum of risk that these poor people would come to expect support and fall into the decadence of ongoing dependency and pauperism. The motto was *laissez faire*. Government intervention and public relief would make charity impersonal; it would create a cumber-some and inefficient bureaucracy; it would be prone to political abuse and corruption. If government were to become involved at all, it would provide business with the wherewithal to create jobs through government loans and tax relief.

Within this context it becomes more understandable that Hoover was successful in the dispersement of private funds before his election and that he was immobilized in the use of public monies as president. The mechanism of relief for the most part remained private, "efficient," free of so-called political corruption and completely unable to deal with the magnitude of the suffering and despair during the Hoover administration.

If Hoover's background made him an unlikely villain in the depression, Roosevelt's background made him an unlikely hero. He was the son of the vice president of several corporations whose wealth spanned generations. His mother was 28 years old and his father was 54 when Franklin was born. He was the only child of this marriage and enjoyed the indulgence of tutors, governesses, foreign travel, sailboats, playmates from his own social class and the best education that money could buy. He went to Groton school, Harvard University and Columbia Law School. Although he dropped out of law school before completing the program, he passed the bar and was accepted to practice in a prestigious New York City law firm. He quickly became interested in politics and became a delegate to the New York Democratic convention in 1910. At that time the Hudson Valley communities, like Hyde Park, were so overwhelmingly Republican that Democratic nominations for state office were given to any delegate who would pay his own way to the convention. In that way Roosevelt was nominated for state senator in 1910, a bad year for Republicans. This, together with Franklin's innate ability as a politician and his well-known family name, resulted in his election. He quickly became part of the liberal Democratic establishment in the legislature and was a typical progressive reformer.

As Hoover was wedded to ideology, Roosevelt was divorced from it. Notwithstanding his progressive ties, his early career could hardly be characterized as committed to social reform. In 1912 he distinguished himself in the Democratic campaign and he was appointed Secretary of the Navy. At this post he showed a flair for administration without the encumberance of rigid adherence to regulations. He was an energetic, colorful and extremely likeable person who was perceived as able to cut through "red tape." In 1920, Roosevelt's talents were engaged by the party by making him the vice presidential candidate on the ticket with James M. Cox. Harding won the election and Roosevelt returned to private life for a time.

During the campaign, some of his statements, while they reflected *real politik*, tended to be interpreted as cynicism. One example of this had to do with his support of the League of Nations as a modality for the preservation of the integrity of small nations. When questioned about the fact that the United States could be outvoted by the small nations, he reassured the questioner that we could easily control the votes of Latin American countries. The press widely reported these statements as hypocritical.

A very sympathetic biographer, Frances Perkins, Roosevelt's Secretary of Labor and a social worker, also suggested that Roosevelt had little real concern about the social reforms that became part of his administration at the beginning of his career (Perkins, 1946, pp. 10–11). He seemed arrogant and supercilious. His imposing height and habit of throwing his head back to peer through pince-nez glasses gave him an appearance of snobbishness. This, together with his affiliation with political reform groups, earned him the contempt of many regular democrats, particularly those of Tammany Hall who saw themselves in the mold of the "common man."

In 1921 Roosevelt was stricken with polio. His return to public life in spite of paralysis was an act of indisputable personal courage. His supporters saw in him a spiritual transformation that supposedly came from the suffering. They claimed that he developed humility, warmth and understanding of adversity that aligned him with the underprivileged. Others were not convinced that this was demonstrated by his actions, philosophy or interest in social reform in the 1920s (Hofstadtler, 1948, p. 323). Nonetheless the image persisted and Roosevelt did nothing to dissuade those convinced of its truth. He was forgiven his aristocratic origins and he was able to align himself with the regular Democrats who earlier had opposed him. In 1924 Roosevelt made a nominating speech for Al Smith. He was on crutches, thin and pale, and struggled to the podium able to muster a smile only when he reached and could grasp the security of the rostrum (Perkins, 1948, p. 37). The famous "Happy Warrior" speech that followed moved the audience and established Roosevelt as potentially a major force in the Democratic Party. In 1928 he again addressed the convention eloquently. Following the convention, Smith promoted Roosevelt as his successor as governor of New York. Roosevelt won that election as well as the presidential election in 1932.

As governor, and early in his presidency, Roosevelt's positions were not very different from Hoover's. In fact, he accused Hoover of being a spendthrift at one time. However, his eloquence and charm reassured a nation groping for leadership. It was his manner that was in sharp contrast to the rather colorless Hoover. Yet, as it became evident that greater action was required, Roosevelt's ideological flexibility allowed him to reverse his position and follow the direction of those who prodded him toward social reform, the direction given by this social work advisors.

Roosevelt clearly was not a social worker. His identity was that of a pragmatic politician who, by the time he reached the presidency, was closely aligned with the bosses of Tammany Hall. Considering their history, Roosevelt should have been the antithesis of what the social workers would support. Just the opposite was the case. From the early days of his New York legislative experience, strong relationships grew between him and social workers such as Frances Perkins and Harry Hopkins. They were the settlement workers, the activists, not the Charity Organization people. It was these people who would provide the direction that Roosevelt would follow more and more as the New Deal matured. Of these social workers and their impact it was said:

> Hull House, Henry Street, The Consumer's League, and the other organizations educated a whole generation in social responsibility. Henry Morgenthau Jr., Herbert Lehman, and Adolph A. Berle, Jr., all worked at Henry Street; Frances Perkins, Gerard Swope, and Charles A. Beard at Hull House, (where John Dewey was an early member of the board of trustees); Sidney Hillman at both Hull House and Henry Street; Joseph B. Eastman at Robert A. Wood's South End House in Boston; an Iowa boy coming east from Grinell College in 1912 went to work at Christadora House on the lower east side of New York: His name, Harry Hopkins. Through Belle Moskowitz the social work ethos infected Alfred E. Smith; through Frances Perkins and others, Robert F. Wagner; through Eleanor Roosevelt, active in the women's trade union league and a friend of Florence Kelley's and Lillian Wald's, Franklin D. Roosevelt.

> And, for all the appearance of innocence, and defenselessness, the social workers' apparatus wielded power. "One could not over-estimate" observed Wagner, "the central part played by social workers in bringing their representatives in congress and state legislatures the present and insistent problems of modern day life." The subtle and persistent saintliness of the social workers was, in the end, more deadly than all of the bluster of business. Theirs was the implacability of gentleness (Schlessinger, 1957, p. 25).

Because of his alliance with these progressive social workers, Roosevelt experienced rejection and vituperation from business leaders and the wealthy. He had not expected this. Although he had experimented with novel approaches to setting right the economy and occasionally engaged in anti-business rhetoric, he felt that his initial program had protected the vested interests of business. As the depression wore on, however, greater and greater pressures began to be felt by the administration from labor and form the left. The Townsend movement and Huey Long's "share the wealth" movement threatened Roosevelt's basic power base. With the "Hate Roosevelt" posture of business he was inclined to move even more clearly toward the left and, by 1935, he was calling for a redistribution of wealth, bitterly attacking the "special interests," thoroughly committed to deficit spending, and strongly supporting definitive and strong labor legislation such as the Wagner Act. The settlement social workers had become his closest advisers.

Roosevelt's strengths were suited to the times. He reflected the popular opinion better than any politician before or since. He had charm and self-assuredness. When Hoover told people that "prosperity was just around the corner," Hoover believed it and sounded like a hypocrite. When Roosevelt said "There is nothing to fear but fear itself," he recognized it as a palliative but followed the statement with experimentation and action, if not direction, so that examples could be drawn to support the eloquent promise that people were so anxious to believe.

The fierce loyalties that Roosevelt had from and for his friends and associates were another great resource to him. This was particularly true in social welfare. His lack of ideological commitment thus became his stength as Hoover's philosophical consistency was a weakness. He was not concerned with labels. He tried to weave different positions together, even if rationally they were opposed. Pragmatic proof was all that mattered, except for practical feasibility. Finally, as Hoover had been unlucky in every respect while president, Roosevelt was blessed with good fortune that almost gave credence to a premise of divine guidance. From the election in 1910 to World War II, events propelled Roosevelt into the role of respected leader where he seemed flawlessly to fulfill the expectations of the majority of people.

If this was true for the general population it was more true of social workers. To them Roosevelt's activities were the embodiment of their reform orientation from the inception of their profession. Never mind their support in previous decades for rugged individualism, social Darwinism, *Laissez Faire,* and the benevolence of wealth—the very foundations of the Hoover perspective. Never mind the covert sabotage and denigration of so-called wholesale reform. Those were things of the past. These notions could be viewed as still true and applicable but only in different contexts. Social work had been misunderstood. It had always maintained and sometimes supported a nucleus of activists within the profession. The leadership of this group was now engaged in the highest echelons of government. They enjoyed the support of their professional associates. In exchange, the profession would acquire the image of an active and creative force within the leadership of the nation.

The New Deal Social Workers

Frances Perkins and Harry Hopkins were the major social work advisers in the Roosevelt administration. They and those who worked with them fashioned the social services programs of the New Deal. They quickly lost their quality of uniqueness in the profession. They led the way as social work turned away from its traditional concerns with pauperism, individualism, and the other shibboleths of Charity Organization Society. Social activism became the mainstream of the profession. The surviving idealistic remnants of the social workers of the progressive era came forth from the sanctuary of the settlement houses and into the role of professional leadership. The backgrounds of these administration social workers will now be studied together with the thrust of social work as it mirrored their ideas (Schlessinger, 1959, pp. 198–300, 263–266).

Frances Perkins' background, at first glance, made her as unlikely a candidate for reformer as was Roosevelt's. She grew up in Worcester, Massachusetts and received her education at Mt. Holyoke. She then went to Chicago and joined the staff of Hull House. After a time she went to Philadelphia to study economics with a reform oriented scholar, Simon Patten. Now thoroughly committed to reform, she became executive secretary of the Consumer's League, Florence Kelly's agency, in 1910. In that position she entered the field of political activism, became close to many New York politicans including Robert Wagner, Al Smith, Tammany's Big Tim Sullivan, and Franklin Roosevelt. Perkins became part of a group of social workers who were active in New York politics and who were known as the "dedicated old maids" (although Perkins was married in 1913).

From the beginning, her ability, strength, and articulate intelligence gave her enormous influence. After the famous fire at the Triangle Shirtwaist factory in 1911, Perkins, who actually saw the fire, was named secretary to a citizens' committee on safety. She also served as an investigator for a commission set up by the state legislature in response to the tragedy. Her prowess as a lobbyist was demonstrated by her activities in the education of Robert Wagner and Al Smith about factory conditions:

In June, 1911 [the New York State Legislature] set up a factory investigating commission. Its chairman was Robert F. Wagner, an earnest young German from the upper East Side, who had become Democratic leader in the Senate; Al Smith, the Irishman, was vice chairman. Both Smith and Wagner understood from their own experience something of the helplessness of the immigrant laborers in American industry.

Yet neither Wagner nor Smith had fully realized before the aching hours of labor in dark lofts, the filth and stink in the washrooms and toilets, the callous use of child labor. Frances Perkins, as an investigator for the commission, took Smith to see the thousands of women, pale and exhausted, coming off the 10 hour night shift on the rope walk in Auburn. In one factory she made Bob Wagner crawl through the tiny hole in the wall, marked "Fire Escape," to the steep iron ladder covered with ice and ending 12 feet above the ground. She got the commission up at dawn to watch 6 and 7 year old children snipping beans and shelling peas at a Cattaraugus County cannery. Neither Smith nor Wagner ever forgot what he then learned (Schlessinger, 1957, p. 96).

Perkins went on to become director of investigations of the State Factory Commission, chair of the State Industrial Board, and was Industrial Commissioner for Franklin Roosevelt when he was governor of New York. When Roosevelt was elected to the presidency in 1932, he named Perkins Secretary of Labor, the first woman cabinet member in United States history. She served through the administration. Her intense relationship with Roosevelt was demonstrated during her attempt in 1944 to resign just before Roosevelt's final inauguration. Although he accepted her resignation at first, he dragged his heels at naming a successor (Perkins, pp. 391–393). Finally he emotionally asked her to stay on.

Unlike Frances Perkins, Harry Hopkins came from a working class background. He frequently referred to himself as "the son of a harness maker from Sioux City." This romantic self-identification coupled with his brusque and irreverent speech and manner, his dishevelled appearance, and the fact that he spoke quickly out of the side of his mouth with an air of cockiness gave him a "Runyonesque" facade. He graduated from Grinnell College and took a summer job at Christadora House, a settlement in New York City. There he was profoundly moved by the conditions of the poor. His sister, Adah Aime, was, at the time, registrar of the New York School for Philanthropy and a former associate of Jane Addams (Hopkins, p. 4). She probably had considerable influence on the direction his career took.

Hopkins became well known as a social work administrator early in his career. He began a regular job with the Association of Improving the Condition of the Poor. In 1915 he became Executive Secretary of the Board of Child Welfare in New York City. From 1917 to 1922 Hopkins worked as director of the regional offices of the American Red Cross in New Orleans and Atlanta. He then became the director of the New York Tuberculosis Health Association who "loaned" him to the New York State Temporary Emergency Relief Administration under Governor Roosevelt in 1931. He was so effective that when, in 1933, Roosevelt wished to appoint him as the head of the newly legislated Federal Emergency Relief Administration (FERA), Governor Lehman of New York was disinclined to let him go.

In the end Hopkins did become a part of the Roosevelt administration. Hopkins held to some aspects of the social work charity philosophy. He believed very strongly in the notion that the acceptance of relief was degrading to the recipient (Hopkins, pp. 101–109). Furthermore he felt that only those who were in dire need should receive assistance (Schlessinger, 1959, p. 267). For these reasons the FERA was seen only as a temporary measure and included a rigid means test. It was soon replaced by the various work programs that were more characteristic of the New Deal.

The minimizing of the so-called humiliating effect of relief was the motive of other aspects of the Hopkins program. In addition to the self-respect of the "job" related to work relief and local administration, the monies were dispensed in cash rather than in the commonly used requisition or "relief in kind," which specified items that could be purchased (Ibid., p. 104). Forcing the person to obtain "what he needed" was seen by Hopkins as degrading. Allowing him or her to choose for himself or herself was seen as enhancing dignity. Furthermore work relief was soon replaced by W.P.A. or C.W.P.A. where the worker received wages, albeit minimum wages, for hours worked rather than a grant for his needs as assessed by a social worker. Hopkins also suggested counseling for those who because of age or infirmity had to be pensioners. This counseling would enable them to maintain their dignity in spite of their dependency.

The keystone of the Hopkins philosophy was the idea that the Depression could be relieved by spending rather than by cutting budgets. This was in sharp contrast to the previous administration. Hopkins felt the supplies of money had been locked up in government and the pockets of the very wealthy. Relief and the spending of money by the poor therefore would have enabled the government to save the nation's economy. This concept was one of redistribution of wealth and of encouraging the circulation of currency.

Other social work professionals quickly took advantage of the renown of Hopkins and Perkins. In calling for professional standards in both the public and private sectors of social work, Stanley Davies wrote about the opportunity to enhance their influence:

> If social workers are sufficiently flexible to see their opportunity they will also be in the forefront when it comes to the organization, development of standards, and direction of public relief. It is a time when governing officials, having been made aware of their responsibility for the mitigation of suffering, are unsure and perplexed. It is a time when many such officials are prepared as never before to listen to the man that knows, who speaks with the authority of experience, and who can show the way. In other words, it is a time of rare opportunity for social workers who will assert themselves and seize their chance to utilize their professional equipment in behalf of the million of human beings who must be aided (Davies, p. 438).

Edith Abbott did seize upon the opportunity to promote her progressive thinking. If social work was to engage in public social services, it needed to promote a redirection of the thinking about poverty (Abbott, 1934, pp. 1–16). Abbott suggested that the old kind of thought was a reflection of the Malthusian theory which held the view that the poor were poor by virtue of their own inadequacies. This view was reflected in the so-called pauper laws that were still on the books in many states in the 1930s. They continued to exist because of the indifference of social workers to welfare legislation with the very few in government being the exception. Abbott pressed for more and more involvement of social workers in the political arena.

As early as 1932 the governor of Pennsylvania, reflecting the attitudes of some of the other liberal politicians of the time, heaped praise upon the profession (Pinchot, pp. 90–96). Social workers were exorted to lead the nation in a new era of public responsibility:

> It is a time, if ever there was a time, for real progress to be made in the social work field. Energetic and intelligent leadership can and should direct an already aroused public interest along the line of a forward moving social program. Opportunity, in the guise of popular attention to your ideas, is pounding on your door.
>
> I am not speaking of progress in the sense of direct and immediate relief of today's sufferers. You know, as well as I know, the tremendous size of that task. You have all done yeoman service along that line. But it is a line of defense not of attack. Our battle against unemployment and all the other evils and tragedies of an industrial society can never be won by the defensive tactics alone.

The progress I mean is a more permanent sort of progress. It is the progress of prevention instead of cure, of attack instead of defense. It is progress toward the goal of a better social order in an industrial nation and industrial world. As I see it, that goal can only be achieved by the expression of a new national philosophy of social work. It must come through active realization that the welfare of the working people in good times and bad cannot be left to the occasional benevolence of the wealthy—that the workers' welfare is the solemn responsibility of society as a whole. In short, social work is properly a national responsibility and a national duty (Ibid., p. 91).

The praise grew out of social work's apparent turnabout the previous year. Recognizing the imminent collapse of the private charity movement, the National Conference of Social Work in 1932 aligned itself to the growing liberal movement. Delegates to the conference expressed a view that aid should be public and the federal government should become the major source of funds for the needy (Leiby, p. 221). The conference dedicated itself to public welfare in 1933, with the general sessions being totally devoted to the Depression, poverty, and the apparent new era.

There was also a recognition that the credit being given to social workers was perhaps not completely deserved. The actions of the profession needed to more closely approximate the perceptions of those who praised them. Rather than making substantive changes in the profession, efforts were suggested to promote social work to the public by creating an image, so as to maximize the crest of popularity. The emphasis upon material relief rather than casework was discussed as a technique for appealing to the public's sense of duty.

As social work grew in popularity and influence, it sought to promote its material and rehabilitative programs. Articles gave direction and encouragement to support and participate in the new government involvement in charity work (Abbott, 1936, pp. 396–412). Previously there had been a taboo about social work involvement in the political arena. Welfare job appointments, when they were involved in politics, often were identified as corrupt, particularly in the area of distribution of grants. The new order, however, could be maintained free of this element by a civil service system enhanced by the involvement of professional social workers whose expertise would assure the application of grants to meet existing needs. The professional ethics would act to maintain an honest system. A large number of papers were delivered and written extolling social casework involvement in the public arena. Methods for modification and application of casework and other social work methodology in public and social services abounded.

Those in private agencies followed suit. While acknowledging their inadequacies in providing relief, they attempted to carve a niche for themselves in casework and the maintenance of standards for the entire profession. They stressed that all social work played a role in a new era. It was to be a unified profession. From this source also came a warning that, while government was meeting needs during the emergency, it might not be willing to do so during better times. Poverty, while not as extensive in better times, always existed and required attention (Mandel, pp. 456–464). This prophetic paper suggested that such attention could not be as dependent upon public opinion as government needed to be. It was important to maintain private sources of charity to meet needs when poverty became less popular.

The fear of abandonment by the government was shared by another significant group of social workers, the radicals. They were against over-dependence upon capitalist government for meeting the needs of the poor. Their views differed dramatically in some respects from the mainstream New Deal members of the profession. Their opinions, growth and eventual dubious acceptance of the main aspects of the New Deal had impact upon the element of social reform in social work.

The Radical Social Workers of the Depression

The 1930s are sometimes called "the Red Decade" (Lens, pp. 297–396). During this period, in addition to the preeminence of the liberal left wing of the Democratic Party, various groups far more radical also came to prominence. Frances Townsend would woo the elderly with a program of $200 per month pension to be financed by a $20 billion taxation act. Other pension schemes spoke to varying amounts of benefits and various tax schemes for raising money. More far-reaching plans proposed government ownership and redistribution of wealth, some based on notions of utopian society. One of the most popular programs was the "share the wealth" ideas of Huey P. Long.

With his roots in American populism, Long directly attacked capitalism and demanded a "redistribution of wealth." His dynamic leadership attracted enormous support and gained total control of his state, including agencies of social control. Historians characterized him as a corrupt self-serving demagogue endangering the mechanisms of democracy (Schlessinger, 1960, pp. 42–68). Considering his assassination and the usual problems for popular American anti-capitalist politicians, it is doubtful that he would have enjoyed any political success, or even his limited longevity, without exercising enormous control in his constituency. Certainly the power that he wielded caught the attention of the American power structure.

Within the context of more "normal" political institutions of the

United States, two parties of the left with some power evolved: Norman Thomas' Socialist Party of America and the Communist Party of America, led by Earl Browder. While in some mayoralty races these parties were able to show some strength, particularly in urban areas, their political success was limited in terms of election victories. During this period, however, the communists were able to mobilize large groups of blacks toward political action by championing civil rights.

Social workers had their left-wing counterparts. Since social reform issues became the major concern of the profession, this group became influential during the 1930s. In 1933, Karl Borders of the League for Industrial Democracy was invited to address the national conference of social work. The league was a socialist organization founded by Upton Sinclair and Jack London (Lens, op. cit.).

Borders' basic position was that social workers should automatically be radicalized by their experiences:

> My thesis is a simple and, I believe, a logical one. In a word it is this: "No intelligent social worker can fail to be concerned with the whole social and economic order in which his work is set. The logical pursuit of such a concern will, in the best sense of the word, bring him out a political and economic radical.

> You must be among the leaders of this revolt. Yours is the burden of knowledge. Shout from the housetops, breathe through the written page, and whisper at every board meeting that you will no longer administer to the festering sores of society, which builds skyscrapers upon the roofs of hovels, flaunts riches in the face of poverty, condemns men to beggary while tools rust in the factories—that you will not serve the victims of the idiocy unless at the same time you can share in the building of the world in which these things cannot be. Only in such a program can you do your whole, full rounded duty. Only in such a passion can you find any real self-justification for your weary days of binding up the tragic wounds of mankind" (Borders, pp. 590, 593, 595–596).

Social work was viewed as supporting a system that oppressed the poor, so long as it played a role in capitalist social programs. Participation in total change of the system would provide true help for clients, even for radicals among social workers in the 1930s. This was a position far ahead of its time. The argument resurfaced in the 1970s as the apparent decline of liberal programs took shape when these programs failed to meet their objectives.

In general, the bulk of the left wing of social work supported the new government programs. The New Deal was viewed as democracy fulfilled by many of these social workers. The fact that there were social workers in the executive cabinet was a sign that the profession had achieved national status.

The 1934 National Conference found itself examining the role of social work in government. The radicals raised questions about whether government and social work support of government would be able to truly meet the needs of the poor. While supporting the programs of the New Deal, Mary Van Kleeck, a researcher at the Russell Sage Foundation, keynoted the concerns. She pointed out that in official statements, social workers not only supported government legislation in principle, but identified itself totally with its methods and program. Van Kleeck asked the question:

> whether this reliance upon government commits social workers to the preservation of the *status quo* and separates them from their clients, leading them into the position of defense of the politican in their efforts to protect political institutions against the strains put upon them by the failures of industry to maintain employment, or by the industrial policy which seeks to sustain profits at the expense of standards of living (Van Kleeck, 1934, pp. 473–85).

Van Kleeck pointed to two concepts of government. One, often accepted by social workers, is that "government stands above conflicting interests, and a democracy can be brought by majority vote to decide between those two conflicts and compel standards and policies which are in the public interest" (Ibid., p. 475). Social workers, within the context of these beliefs, had been developing non-partisan reform programs and through lobbying hoping for their adoption by various parties. This, it was hoped, would lead to the enactment of laws that were administered by a government representing the people.

An alternative view of government suggested by Van Kleeck is that it was dominated by the strongest economic interests and became the instrument of those interests. Van Kleeck argued that the experience of the relief program supports this latter theory. Laws which were not in the interest of property or placed large burdens upon property, even if enacted, tended to be in constant jeopardy as property interest pressured government administrators.

The ultimate burden, then, is not for the enactment of a program, but its administration. Social workers, therefore, must maintain vigilance as programs go into effect, and join forces with other workers to pressure for appropriate implementation. The goals of social work and labor were seen as the same, namely, the maintenance of an adequate standard of living for workers and community (Van Kleeck, 1934, pp. 284–303). This goal would be accomplished by developing a new order based on collectivism. The professions would lead such an order, managing industry because of their skills. "But management of industry which can force its policies through because it represents distant owners who have all the power should not continue to control. It must step aside in American life" (Ibid., p. 302). This view was not a rarity. Although not the mainstream of the American Association of Social Workers, it was represented by a "rank and file" group (Fisher, 1936, pp. 5–10).

The Rank and File Movement

The rank and file movement grew out of the social workers' discussion club of New York in 1930 with its roots in the Jewish Federation. It reacted to the Depression and, more importantly, to the apparent failure of social work to adjust its thinking to the crisis of the Depression. During the 1932 National Conference of Social Work there was contact between the members of the New York group and others with similar interests. The result was the formation of similar discussion groups in Boston, Philadelphia, and Chicago (Spano, pp. 68–69).

The two broad areas of concern were the working conditions of social workers and the social conditions of the Depression. The issue of working conditions was dealt with in terms of support for an alliance between social workers and the labor movement. The social issues of concern included unemployment, public relief, social insurance, civil rights, possibilities of war, fascism, and mental hygiene and social chaos. The New York group continued in leadership and in March 1934 published the first issue of a journal called *Social Work Today* which was to speak for the movement. In February, 1935, 30 rank and file groups met at a convention in Pittsburgh and formalized the organization. By 1936 many groups, including some chapters of the mainstream organizations, had units representing the rank and file movement. The character of the organization by that time involved:

> protective organizations in about 35 public agencies in 15 large cities, a dozen Pennsylvania counties, half a dozen Michigan counties and several Ohio counties; in protective organizations in Jewish agencies in five cities; in open forums in over half a dozen cities; in practitioner groups; in three chapters of the American Association of Social Workers, and case workers councils in half a dozen family agencies, in organized activity at the National Conference of Social Work and the National Conference of Jewish Worker Service; in the National Coordinating Committee

of rank and file groups and social work; and in the publication of *Social Work Today*. The total membership of the groups participating in the movement is about 15,000 of whom about 12,000 are members of the 17 organizations affiliated with the National Coordinating Committee. The great majority are employed in public relief agencies (Fisher, 1936, p. 5).

Mary Van Kleeck and Bertha Reynolds became pillars of the board of directors of the journal, and in 1937 Frank Bancroft, a social worker turned reporter, became the paid managing editor of *Social Work Today*. The movement flourished until World War II when it seemed to have lost momentum and enthusiasm (Leiby, 1978, p. 243). It continued to champion social workers in labor unions by supporting the unions incorporating them: the American Federation of State and County municipal employees (AFL) and the United Office & Professional Workers and United Public Workers of America (CIO) (Ibid.). In these organizations the basic conern was with wages and working conditions of social workers. Little, if any, attention was paid to the vital social issues that concerned the original rank and file movement.

Reynolds saw four areas where *Social Work Today* and the movement dealt with issues that were not included in other professional social work journals:

1. Reportage on world events affecting social work and the growth of workers' movements everywhere;
2. Relief and welfare measures and first-hand case illustrations of the way these were working throughout the country;
3. Growth of organization of social workers and the affiliation of such professional unions with the labor movement;
4. Professional content of theory and practice (Reynolds 1969, p. 177).

While a complete coverage of the subject matter in the journal goes far beyond this study, the basic position in each of the four areas will give some picture of the tenets of the rank and file movement.

In the international arena, *Social Work Today* dealt with the situation of the Nazi and fascist states in Europe. Issues of particular concern to social workers were reviewed. Apparently pre-fascist Europe had a strong social work community that was undermined and used by fascist elements (Schlauch, 1935, pp. 14–15).

Through the efforts of European social workers, the plight of those imprisoned in Germany came to the attention of the world. The professional condemnation and efforts to publicize the conditions of prisoners by the underground were reported at length in *Social Work Today*

(Rosenfeld, 1935, pp. 18–19). The journal also reported on repressed members of the profession who were in Germany. Many became refugees. The rank and file organization early on collected and dispersed money through an organization called Hospites to aid these social workers (Cahard, 1937, p. 25).

The state of social welfare in Germany during the Nazi years was the subject of many articles. The true depth of the oppression, however, seemed to escape even these writers. They were able to identify the extortion, the use of programs as an instrument of graft, and the total withdrawal of assistance from the aged, handicapped and sick. Mary Van Kleeck called for social workers to actively oppose Hitler. Other world issues were discussed at length, sometimes with appeals for assistance. They include the Spanish Revolution, the Soviet Revolution, and conditions in Russia from a positive perspective.

Beyond a basic criticism of Nazi regimes, the movement extended its argument to include an appeal for activism. It urged that people who were victims of these regimes be given asylum in the United States. A great deal of effort and space was allotted to this issue. The rank and file movement recognized the Roosevelt administration's reluctance to give sanctuary to those who attempted to escape oppression. In December, 1939 an entire issue of *Social Work Today* was devoted to the plight of displaced people.

The movement also clearly supported peace. It viewed the mobilization effort as a threat to relief and vigorously opposed the draft. National defense was seen as a ploy to increase profits while it drained the American people.

The New Deal also had support as long as the administration did not retreat from its commitment to social programs and relief. When it did, or when any local or state agencies seemed to renege, the journal gave it wide publicity and criticised it severely.

Politically the journal made no bones about its activist/left leanings. It promoted candidates who supported social service programs including Roosevelt (Editorial, 1936, p. 4). It provided a forum for various involved parties to present their social service programs. While it generally opposed Roosevelt as he became heavy handed in regard to welfare, there was total support when he acted in favor of social service programs. Support even extended to approval of his plan to "pack" the Supreme Court.

There was vigorous support for organized labor and representation of social work by organized labor. The strength for effective activism was seen as the potential result of the coalition between labor and the social work professional. One possible strategy was suggested by Mary

Van Kleeck. This was the development of an American Labor Party as a vehicle for true social reform.

In the area of professional practices, a regular feature of the journal was a department known as "Casework Notebook." Within this section were long discussions of casework relationships dealing with clients within the context of reality as perceived by the rank and file movement. It was casework oriented to the problems of the times. Subjects included the effects of poverty on personality, various ways of maintaining client dignity in relief situations, the effect of unemployment on family life, and other issues across the full gamut of social casework practice. Many articles also dealt with psychotherapy, particularly psychoanalysis. In most instances this approach to working with people was treated as detrimental, naive, and ignorant of the real issues that concern people. It also looked upon the psychoanalytic and psychological approach as excusing society for its evils and not fully acknowledging the effect of financial problems on people's personalities.

Gradually the radical movement in social work went the way of many left-wing movements throughout American society. Its anti-war position may have discredited it as the full impact of the war in Europe was felt. Much of the movement was co-opted into the New Deal and the war effort after Pearl Harbor. The prosperity that came after the war made poverty once more an issue alien to the great majority of Americans; poverty again began to be viewed as the problem of minority groups. After the Depression, the groups who had once controlled social work, the private agency therapy people, now no longer encumbered with providing financial assistance, emerged once more to dominate the field. In June, 1942 there was a final edition of *Social Work Today*. It contained no hint that publication would end. The journal simply ceased to exist (Spano, p. 173).

The conservative elements of the profession had greater longevity. Although not in control at the time, they were still a force to be reckoned with during the Depression. They hindered both liberals and radicals. In limited but important areas, they maintained dominance and maintained control of the profession's direction.

Social Work Conservatives During the Depression

The change in philosophical orientation of the field as the New Deal came to power moved the charity organization people out of their preeminence and leadership in the profession. Throughout the history of social work, they had opposed various programs of the more progressive elements of the profession, but had always given lip service to the broad general principles of social reform. They quietly acquiesced to the reform focus of the New Deal, and while they participated in some program development, they generally remained inactive in that arena. Their political position was a promotion of unity in the profession, despite some political differences amongst its members. The fact that different social workers thought differently could provide checks and balances in their performance of professional services in all spheres.

While there seemed to be some change in philosophical orientation, this shift in focus did not become inconsistent with nor force the conservatives to disregard their original interest in technique and therapy. Now no longer involved with organizing charity, since this was a function taken over by government rather than private agencies, they addresses themselves to organizing families in psychological disarray. In 1930 the Charity Organization Society became the Family Service Association, an agency specializing in counseling and casework therapy.

Poverty had become so widespread that it could no longer be looked upon as a disease to be cured by a social worker. "Normal" people were now in need of assistance. Caseworkers were not long in finding the need in their clients for case work services. If there was no need to "rehabilitate" the pauper or "investigate" the application, the case work process could be applied to the alleviation of the apparent psychological distress of poverty (Allen, pp. 333–346).

Case workers, because of their professional training, were seen as ideal administrators of relief. They would sympathize with the client, destigmatize the relief situation, understand the emotional component of the client finding himself or herself without means, without having to request assistance. Indeed, the field needed to deepen its understanding of psychoanalysis so that the unconscious conflicts that surfaced during an emotional crisis could be identified and worked through.

The client needed to be reassured through the case work relationship that he or she had a right to assistance and need not feel humiliated because of his or her dependency. A post-depression training pamphlet for public assistance workers reviewed in detail the required sensitivities of social workers in relief agencies (Towle, 1945). These included an understanding of the effects of asking for help based upon the symbolic meaning of money, unemployment and employment, the personal inadequacy implied in the loss of job, and the denigration in the admission of failure. The professional training that was to be provided to those who were preparing to enter the public welfare agencies would come straight from the case work model. The ground was prepared for the advocacy, the lobbying skills, and the ability to plan and promote legislation and programs for government. New social workers entering the profession would be encouraged to address themselves to the alleged need for the amelioration of the psychological implications of financial deprivation and dependency.

The schools of social work had retained the facilities and philosophies of the older order. Here support for public social services was mainly verbal. The actions supported the long entrenched case work model. Long into the 1940s and beyond, appeal after appeal was made for more adequate preparation of students to serve in public welfare. The schools of social work attempted to convince their critics that there was an inclusion of relevant social welfare material in the curriculum. However, they asserted that the basic case work content was sufficient to train potential welfare administrators (American Association of Schools of Social Work, pp. 170–171). The critics, however, insisted:

> The school should make greater efforts to prepare students to understand the social and economic forces which have such profound effects upon the service programs and to understand public officials and others who represent these forces in the community. "The importance of public relations" and "knowing how to work with politicians" were phrases frequently quoted by those whom the study staff interviewed. The end result of the two year professional course should be students grounded not only in skill and method of getting "things done," but also in the factual basis for understanding psychological, political, and economic factors which may make or break the program. The practitioner needs not only professional competence; he needs perspective and understanding that enable him to function as a member of the profession in a changing world (Ibid., p. 219).

The issue of generic versus specific training of social workers took a new twist. The more progressive view was that education in the area of casework *per se* was looked upon as a speciality, while broader areas such as public welfare needed to be included in a truly "generic" curriculum (McMillan, 1933, pp. 631–638).

In 1933 A. Wayne McMillan was critical of both agencies and schools. Agencies did not subscribe to the need for education as a necessary prerequisite for personnel. This led educators to view the public agency workers and executives as ignorant and incompetent. Thus each party felt that time and effort should not be wasted on the other (Ibid., pp. 632–633). Agencies perceived students who had graduated as really untrained until their employment began. At this time, their sophistication in social work matters could be nurtured through experience and on the job training. The general aura was one of intransigence and mutual contempt.

> Until recently many of the schools have been distressingly ignorant about the field of public welfare. They have envisaged it as a public pasture—a happy hunting ground for bestowers of patronage. . . . This attitude has been reflected in their curriculums, which have tended to concentrate on techniques at the expense of knowledge. If their students were to be assured of respectable jobs in orthodox private charities, the schools had to immerse them in case work methods as viewed from every point of the compass. Little time was left to learn the entire field of public welfare—local, state, and federal. Curriculums with such dispro-portionate emphasis may have produced trained social workers, but they did not produce educated social workers. If this situation had continued, it might ultimately have been desirable to make a distinction in ter-minology, using the title "trained social worker" for those drilled in case work and reserving the title "educated social worker" for those, in addi-tion to case work training with ample amount of supervised field work, had also received a comprehensive knowledge of the field of public welfare and a basic familiarity with research methods (Ibid., p. 633).

There was clearly a coalition and unity between the conservative private agencies and the schools of social work. The pattern seemed to continue with students more able to perform the duties of specific private agencies than to become community public welfare leaders and function within the public welfare structure (Sztz, p. 103).

The variation between schools was enormous in curricular attention to public welfare. It seemed that different schools had developed specializations in a variety of social work practices. Only the Chicago School was viewed as concentrating in public welfare social work as well as in research. This school provided paid faculty supervision within public welfare agencies for student field placement. There would therefore be no arguments about the inferiority of supervision of students by "untrained" agency personnel. This idea was first in-troduced in 1928 by Edith Abbott. Many years later, as schools became more involved with providing better experiences in public welfare and other non-traditional placements, this method was the basis for field supervision. The changes were not to occur for several decades.

A great deal of classroom emphasis during the periods seemed to shift away from public welfare concerns of the apparent mainstream of social work practice. While Edith Abbott and the other Chicago people were looking for ways to integrate their curriculum with the needs of the time, other schools became preoccupied to the point of obsession with the struggle between Rankian or Freudian approaches to case work treatment. The Rankian or functional school seemed to emphasize not a broadening of the educational experience provided in existing programs, but denigrating this education. Case work education was not solely a "learning" process, it needed also to be a "growth" process, i.e., a process directing itself toward emotional insight and readjustment.

In spite of the poverty and suffering of the Depression, alleviation of these evils seemed to escape the attention of most of the social work educators. Rather, they focused on developing ways for readjusting the personalities of their students so that they would achieve psychological health to perform their professional duties in therapy. The effect, discussed in early chapters, drew the professionals and ultimately the profession out of the area of social reform.

Committees set up by the American Association of Schools of Social Work became battlegrounds for the partisans of the case work versus public welfare controversy. In 1931 Virginia Robinson resigned the position she held on one such committee during the middle of deliberations. The committee's report indicated consensus of case work issues such as the need for enhancement of the worker/client relationship, but showed a wide divergence of opinion about the need in education for theoretical, historical and non-psychologically oriented methodology (Hellenbrand, 1965, p. 263.) Later committees had problems in securing casework participants. Those interested in change participated, and committee membership was weighted toward the public welfare perspective. The reports and their conclusions and recommendations could thus be easily ignored by uninvolved case workers as the professional school moved more and more toward a more thorough therapeutic orientation.

The content of case work courses stressed the feelings the client had about his life experiences. The feelings about external reality were rooted in life experiences and relationships early in life (Ibid., p. 270). Much of the focus of the relationship was in this area rather than upon the tribulations of living in an economic depression.

Heavy emphasis on the concept of resistance as a natural phenomenon was presented in case work classes. Case work theory suggested that there was a natural inclination to avoid dealing with "real" problems. A person would thus be inclined to deny "real" problems because they were too painful to face, suggested personal failure, threatened to conjure up other unconscious material, and were contrary to a natural inclination to avoid change in behavior. Personality change seemed possible only during a severe crisis. A crisis such as unemployment or needing relief was looked upon in many ways as a blessing in disguise. The resistance of the client manifested itself in his or her inclination to blame external factors for personal problems. Thus it was clear that the "real problem" existed within the client. The social worker needed to be aware that the basis of problem-solving might be beyond the client's statement of the problem. To be genuinely helpful, case workers often needed to be trained to go beyond the basic problem that brought the client to the agency. This perspective, of course, minimized the importance of the financial holocaust of the 1930s and the needs it created.

In the agencies the conservatives promoted a notion of psychotherapy as a method of social work that supplemented material assistance. This justified the continuation of training and education in casework technique as the core of in-service training and curricula of schools of social work, and the continued exclusion of material that related to public welfare, despite the cajoling of the professional leadership active in government. This remnant of casework control eventually provided a springboard for the caseworkers to later reestablish their domination of the field. In addition to the liberals, other groups reacted strongly against the continuation of casework as the core of social work education. These included the rank and file and certain student groups.

Reactions Against Conservative Caseworker-Controlled Professional Education

To the rank and file movement, social work education was clearly under the control of private social work. The view was that private social work, and by inference the education that grew out of it, was hopelessly inadequate to meet the needs of the times. Social work education failed to prepare the student for the sheer enormity of the problems faced by the social worker in the public welfare front line. The frustration and disillusionment resulting from lack of funds, intransigent administration, and occasionally physical violence needed to be a subject of discussion. It was suggested that the agency as an institution was at fault. The social worker could be truly helpful to the poor by joining in protest organizations, or even revolution.

Training through agency in-service programs was simply a "routine bag of tricks" rather than genuine professional skills (Reynolds, 1936, p. 10). The person needed to be educated as a whole, acquiring a full range of skills with which to deal with clients. The acknowledged limitations of professional education such as the absence of economic and political content needed to be addressed. It was incumbent upon welfare workers to both educate themselves and press for the content they saw as relevant in the curriculum of schools of social work (Ibid., p. 12).

This position tended to become the preeminent one in the movement. Not only was there pressure for in-service training, but also efforts to promote institutes, part-time schooling, and agency time off for attending schools of social work. Furthermore the rank and file conference laid out other desirable dimensions of the program relevant to their training. These included more content in economics and politics, student involvement in the teaching programs, a recognized student organization, and opportunities for "free discussions" (Ibid., p. 12).

Social Work Today reported on one element in social work education that apparently cannot be found elsewhere, the student movement opposing the casework mainstream of the Depression years. This slow beginning seemed to have little effect on the controversy of the 1930s but would become the core of the social work. Students often have a perspective different than their teachers. Many have had years of experience prior to entering school. As a result, some of the aforementioned discontent with the relevancy of the casework-dominated curriculum played a significant part in the chronic discontent of social work students. This continues to be a student concern to this day. Apparently under the encouragement of the rank and file movement, these issues were raised when the students of the New York School of Social Work were first to organize in 1935. They addressed not only the relevancy issue, but also their high tuition and the failure of the school and the profession to involve themselves in broader social problems (Blair, p. 26).

By 1938 a student organization was formally announced after an informal meeting at the New York School. This group criticized giving adequate training of case work technique but only lip service to public welfare courses. A listing of courses for employed workers, developed in 1938 by the New York School of Social Work, was said not to list "a single course designed primarily to satisfy the education needs of the more than three thousand rank and file social investigators in New York's Department of Welfare" (Dallob, p. 9). A later proposal for education of social workers involved the creation of a union agency school and government cooperative education program at all levels of practice. The program was to encompass in-service training, extension training, and full-time training at a state subsidized university (Committee on Education and Training, p. 6). Although it engaged in early planning stages with the faculty of one school, this program never came to fruition.

It was clear that in spite of early reluctance, the left-wing movement and the students eventually supported professional education. They recognized limitations, but supported the increased availability of professional education to rank and file workers. Their efforts were all directed toward improvement of existing programs rather than a total reorganization of professional education. This was acceptance in name, if not in principle, of the social work education mainstream.

The American Association of Social Work Students was soon founded and consisted of students in 20 of the 32 schools of the time. It affiliated itself with the American Association of Schools of Social Work. This affiliation made the organization a part of the professional mainstream and generally, thereafter, it took a non-confrontive, acquiescent position (Editorial, p. 40). Later during 1938 a letter to the editor proclaimed a student organization at one of the most psychiatrically oriented, conservative schools of social work, the Smith College School of Social Work. Having been in contact with other students who were organized, they took the initiative and organized themselves. ". . . . it was the first meeting ever called by Smith students to consider problems entirely on their own!" Issues involved student problems like scholarships, misinformation, and the desire to have subject areas relevant to social reform included in the curriculum (Leiter, p. 13).

We have seen, therefore, that the control of the schools of social work and their curricula by the caseworkers met with opposition from many groups. While the liberal New Deal workers pressured the schools for more public welfare content, the more radical rank and file group were also sharply critical. Schools, according to the rank and file had curricula that were irrelevant to the problems that the social worker faced from day to day. Nonetheless, they opted to accept the schools as legitimate and support efforts to convince their leadership to expand the scope of the programs to make them meaningful.

Other groups to arise during this period were students' organizations independent of school administration. They too raised some criticisms but chose to affiliate with the American Association of Schools of Social Work and, until the 1960s restricted themselves mainly to non-controversial issues.

Summary

During the Depression, social work had been propelled to national prominence and the profession gained status and respect. The leadership of the profession shifted from the casework-oriented Charity Organization Society workers to the settlement workers aligned with the Roosevelt administration. Nonetheless, the conservative workers retained their control of social work schools and private agencies. From this position they advocated a continuation of the dominance of casework as the major aspect of social work practice. In spite of constant pressure and efforts to convince them otherwise they also retained a casework-dominated curriculum in schools of social work.

During this same period the rank and file movement also developed. They, too, chided the conservatives to give up their casework perspective. In addition, they raised important questions that were far more global than those raised by the liberals. They voiced dismay and promoted professional action against international fascism and Nazism long before others took a stand. They had a strong commitment toward adequate relief for the unemployed and saw themselves as part of the working class. They aligned themselves with the labor movement and became a part of the C.I.O. They equated social work with a socialist perspective and warned against too great a dependence upon government social programs in a capitalist society. Their warnings were prophetic: after the New Deal the status of social programs and social work declined for many of the reasons predicted by the rank and file.

Chapter 8

Reactions and Counterreactions: The Contemporary Period

At the beginning of World War II social workers had established themselves as vital advisers and innovators in government. To the public eye they were the source of innovation that had rescued the United States from the depths of the Depression. Theirs was a philosophy that had shown itself to be appropriate in the industrialized America of the twentieth century. It provided for a redistribution of wealth without the perceived evils of socialism or communism. Their belief was that the dream of a classless society through cooperation and evolution, the Christian Socialism of the Progressive era, had been established (Schlessinger, pp. 367–368, 384–387, 467–468). A consensus had developed in the support of the welfare state. Social workers were both parents and midwives to the new ideas. Yet, those involved in government planning were a minority of the profession. The image of social workers as program innovators was encouraged by those who controlled the profession. This was only a facade. Those who promoted the image clung to their preoccupation with psychotherapeutic "direct services," and gravitated toward practice in the private agencies (Leiby, pp. 270–271). The great social programs conceived by their colleagues were administered by people who, at best, had only marginal identification with the profession.

While the New Deal social work leaders called again and again for educational content relevant to public social services, the professional caseworkers exercised their power over the educational programs to keep them engaged in the training that was appropriate only to private agencies. The result was that as a profession, they were later blamed for whatever failures the social programs were said to have and were despised by those who recognized that social workers had not delivered the resources and services that the programs promised. While they enjoyed prominence because of the general acceptance of the welfare state, they were not involved in the implementation or guidance of the programs. Like Macbeth, they accepted the mantle when they were clothed in borrowed robes and like Macbeth, it was to become their undoing.

The Decline of the Reformers and Radicals of the New Deal Period

Like many of their intellectual contemporaries, most social workers opposed the war prior to the invasion of Pearl Harbor. Their fear, well justified, was that the war would bring with it a halt in the support for social programs. What was not so evident to them was that military service and industry, to support the war effort, would end the unemployment of the Depression. Even less predictable was the unparalleled prosperity that the expanding economy of the post-war period brought. Poverty as a common experience of most American people became a thing of the past. Being poor was relegated mostly to certain segments of the population who, because of race, occupation, or isolation, were not in society's mainstream. These outsiders could be ignored or blamed for their own problems (Leiby, pp. 272–273).

Under administrations subsequent to Roosevelt the responsibility of the government for social services was accepted by presidents of both parties until 1981. The social service administration functions in a newly developing Federal bureaucracy came to be controlled under Roosevelt by the social work liberals. The rewards these liberals received were security in the job and a good salary. They became "professional reformers," planners and government experts (Ibid., pp. 300–301).

From the very beginning these New Deal liberals had been part of the settlement movement but were more clearly related to the Christian Socialist idea of Jane Addams and that of the radical socialists. They all felt that social change and distribution of wealth could occur without revolution or disruption because it was in the best interest of all. Democratic government control through legislation was, in their minds, the key to a workable, managed quasi-capitalist economy.

Satisfied as they were in the government bureaucracy, they became unlikely to criticize or attempt to radically reorganize existing programs. They did try to attempt to expand these programs, but also failed to see the various shortcomings that arose. Where needs were not met because of institutional barriers, they tended to explain it in terms of natural bureaucratic functioning in human service delivery. The response was simply to administer existing programs, ignore all discrepancies between themselves as part of the legitimate government. To those who recognized inequities and attempted to remedy them, there was the threat of sanctions, including loss of position. The sanctions were well demonstrated in the over-all post war reaction to the more left-wing radical group of rank and file social workers.

McCarthyism and the Demise of the Social Work Left

The post-war red scare put an end to the radicalism of the 1930s, in social work and in other areas. As early as 1938, the House of Representatives set up the Committee on Unamerican Activities. It was their job to uncover subversive activities in the United States. In concrete terms, it accomplished little or nothing. What it did do was to gain enormous publicity through innuendo and character assassination, persecute and intimidate people with left-of-center political opinions (Morrison & Commanger, pp. 864–865). The anti-communist agitation created by the committee led to the enactment of the Alien Registration Act (Smith Act) in 1940. This law outlawed advocacy of revolution and embraced doctrines of guilt by intent and guilt by association. The McCarren-Nixon Internal Security Bill of 1950 was even more clearly a sedition act. Passed over President Truman's veto, it required registration of communist front organizations, exclusion of "Communists" from defense industry jobs, deportation of aliens involved with "suspect organizations," and made it illegal to conspire to act in a way that would substantially contribute to creating an American Dictatorship (Ibid., p. 868). Federal employees were required to sign loyalty oaths. Many states followed suit with similar laws that also required loyalty oaths for state employees.

The leading role in the red scare was played by Senator Joseph McCarthy of Wisconsin. In 1950 he alleged that between 57 and 205 state department employees were on a list of communists "in his possession." He never produced the list. He was ". . . a finished demagogue . . . brutally unscrupulous, cunning and adroit, he hoped to achieve power by exploiting the communist issue: his methods were wild charges, faked evidence, innuendoes and lies, appeals to ignorance, prejudice, hatred and fear." (Ibid., p. 867) Other players in this macabre travesty included Richard Nixon, then a congressman, and Attorney General Herbert Brownell. To support this red scare, various trials and convictions around espionage and international intrigue were also carried on. Their content was related to American paranoia about the "loss" of China and the Russian atom bomb.

Organized labor was also under attack. The Taft-Hartley Act enacted in 1947 forbade certain union practices such as secondary boycots, jurisdictional strikes, featherbedding, closed shop, and provided for a

60-day cooling-off period for strikes. The C.I.O. condemned their member unions who were allegedly communist-led in 1946. Under pressure from the Taft-Hartley Act and politics of the time, they expelled those "Communist-led" unions in 1949. One such union expelled was the United Office and Professional Workers of America (UOPWA) of which the social service employees union as well as other social work unions were a part. Following this expulsion, social agencies would neither sign contracts with these unions nor hire social workers who were members of them. This included almost all of the rank and file social workers (Reynolds, p. 273).

The rank and file social workers were heavily unionized. They felt that their philosophy and future required them to become an integral part of organized labor. As a result, the actions against the C.I.O. unions affected them greatly. They also tied themselves to the progressive movement of 1948 and supported the Progressive/American Labor party candidate, Henry Wallace. This involvement also created difficulties for them when that movement was considered to be communist inspired.

By 1947, loyalty oaths had become common-place and their use spread. The association with the expelled unions and Wallace campaign was used to discredit social workers and suggested that they were disloyal. Those who did not resign were given "below average" evaluations, even when previous evaluations had been satisfactory. This was done on the pretext that they were guilty of misconduct or were discrediting their department (Ibid., p. 269).

Further harassment of left-wing social workers by various anti-communist upsurges are widely talked about in professional circles, but little written documentation can be found. Bertha Reynolds, however, speaks at length about her experiences during this period and is a major source of information for this report. Some indication of the limitations of reporting on this period is the fact that while Reynolds reported that Henry Wallace, the Progressive Party candidate in 1948, addressed the Joint Committee of Trade Unions in Social Work at the National Conference of Social Work, (Ibid., p. 292) the speech cannot be found in the conference report. The official conference report ordinarily includes verbatim speeches and papers of significance given at the conference.

Social agencies and social workers functioned as supporters of anti-communist governmental policies in some of their actions. Social workers were harassed by agencies for advocating any kind of action against their employers, including such actions as asking for a raise. Often, agency disciplinary action and dismissal were threatened (Ibid.,

p. 263). Social worker reactions against untruthful press reports about welfare clients were suppressed. The same was true about worker protests about unfair practices toward recipients and other harassment of clients.

In 1946 the American Association of Social Workers conducted a hearing before the state commission of social welfare about practices of the New York City Department of Welfare. The committee was said to be biased and anxious to prove that the Welfare Department had operated appropriately. Employees willing to cooperate with the committee and agency were interviewed in private session and their testimony was recorded. Selected testimony was then read into the record at the hearing with the witnesses simply affirming that the statements were theirs. Only one witness with professional standing made a statement about the absence of professional standards in the department and she was discredited by a number of rehearsed witnesses (Ibid., pp. 267–268). One of the most shameful incidents in the history of social work, involving social workers and social work agencies, occurred during this period of time. The incident occurred in regard to the children of Julius and Ethel Rosenberg. After the execution of their parents, the youngsters were to live with their uncle who had also been the Rosenberg's lawyer. However, the uncle died of a heart attack following the execution. Reynolds reports what occurred soon thereafter:

A foster home of superior advantages had just begun to give them (the children) love and comfort when, at bedtime, it was entered by police officers, an attorney for the department of welfare, and a social worker from a private children's agency, demanding immediate custody of the children on the charge of neglect. The children were sent to an institution away from everyone they knew while the trial of the neglect charge was pending. It took Habeas Corpus proceedings before the Supreme Court of New York State to release them to the care of their aged grandmother as co-guardian with an eminent social worker. Over 250 courageous social workers signed a petition (in spite of threats of reprisal to some of them if they even discussed the case) and hundreds more wrote letters to the court. I was one of the delegation to the mayor, protesting the conduct of the department of welfare. We heard at his office wild charges that the foster parents were communists, the children would be spirited away to Canada if not seized at once, the fund raised by "Uncle Manny" for their education proved that they were being exploited for money, etc. All this added up to two suffering children being used as a political football, with the cooperation of social agencies which should have respected some fundamental principles of social work as the right of next-of-kin to provide for their children. And, if there was just grounds for a charge of neglect such that the children must be removed from a home, to do so with careful preparation and with less trauma than results from a bed-time raid and a police cordon around the house (Ibid., p. 342).

Reynolds herself reported that her outspoken positions created personal difficulties for her. A paper entitled "McCarthyism vs. Social Work" written by her was advertised as being offered at the National Conference of Social Work. Although the content was not known by anyone but the author at the time, Reynolds reports that the title was so frightening to a school of social work that they barred her from a summer seminar. This had occurred even though she was accepted by them and welcomed earlier (Ibid., p. 277). A pamphlet discussing the social work controversy between functional and diagnostic schools written by Reynolds almost was not published. It was said to be too controversial. After great effort, it was finally published by the C.I.O. under the title, *Casework: Advance or Retreat,* in 1949 (Ibid., p. 285).

Social workers were thus faced with alternatives. They could fight and oppose the system and face punitive action or dismissal. Apparently many did. The other alternative was to quietly acquiesce. Practices in welfare departments kept the percentage of social workers with graduate training working for that agency quite low. While 41 percent of the people calling themselves "social workers" were in the employ of welfare departments in 1950, only 4 percent of them had two or more years of training in a graduate school of social work. This compared to 42 percent of the workers in private family services agencies and 83 percent in psychiatric social work (Wilensky & Lebeaux, p. 292).

Later efforts would be made to recruit these professionals to the public assistance agencies through generous stipends, work-study programs, and higher salaries (Ibid.). Nonetheless, the attraction of the private agencies remained. Even when their salaries were lower, the private non-welfare agencies attracted a lion's share of the graduate social workers. These agencies not only were more prestigious but allowed the workers to assist clients without becoming embroiled in dangerous political controversies. They were the safe havens from criticism during the difficult red scare years because they had never become involved with reform. Here, the method of help was and always had been psychotherapy. By 1950, social work practice was almost completely dominated by the practice of therapy. As late as 1969 it was reported that the vast majority of social workers were still employed and being trained for private agencies and the so-called "prestigious" public agencies such as psychiatric hospitals (Kraft, pp. 343–366).

The period of the red scare of the 1950s brought with it the same kinds of reactions in social work that it brought to other professions. Most of the more conservative members of the field remained silent as their colleagues were stripped of their civil rights. Some even participated in the attack against the left wing. Overall, the mainstream social workers pledged themselves to be anti-communist and retreated to casework therapeutical practice. The rank and file and other activists were discredited and purged from the profession. Their issues were submerged and ignored until the social upheavals of the 1960s and 1970s.

The Reemergence of the Issues of Proverty, Social Reform and Social Work and Education

After World War II, when social work retreated into casework treatment, it also received the respect accorded to all professionals in the mental hygiene area. Together with psychiatry, psychology, and school counseling the profession grew and was accepted as a necessary part of the services being offered by various social institutions. The emphasis was upon therapy and technique.

The rapidly expanding programs of public assistance created a number of available jobs for college graduates during the 1950s and 1960s. Many of these jobs paid salaries comparable to teaching and promoted themselves as providing much needed service to an unserved community. Idealistic people wishing to engage in meaningful work and provide necessary assistance to others flocked to the agencies. However, they soon became caught up in mountains of bureaucratic red tape and "paternalistic and stifling supervision." They often found themselves engaging in activities they regarded as punitive and oppressive toward their clients, rather than being helpful (Scott, pp. 131–134).

One available alternative for the disillusioned worker was to take one of the work-study grants from the agencies that had become available. These grants paid for professional social work graduate education for employees of public assistance agencies. In return for the stipend, the social worker agreed to work for the agency for a period of time, usually two years following his or her graduation from graduate school. Many of these people accepting these grants worked their required time and then gravitated to more attractive jobs in psychiatric or private family agencies. Those remaining in public welfare agencies found easy access to administrative and supervisory positions provided they supported agency activities. Thus, stipends, easily available jobs and a ladder for upward mobility caused the field of social work to burgeon during this time (Wilensky & Lebeaux, p. 312).

Little of social reform or content relevant to public programs was offered until well into the 1960s. The assumption was that skilled casework practitioners who had been trained in psychotherapy would rehabilitate the poor and reduce welfare roles. Thus there was a continuation of the concept of pauperism as the psychological explanation of poverty that justified graduate education for professional social workers in welfare departments.

Of particular concern was families that were said to be dependent, multi-problem families. In one study a group of about 6 percent of the families in the community of St. Paul, Minnesota was said to "absorb" over half of the services of the dependency, health, and adjustment agencies (Buell, p. 9).

An additional notion was also promoted. Not only were there "multi-problem" families, but many of these families belong to certain ethnic groups. The thesis was that ethnic groups had not assimilated into American culture. Groups retained their identity and dealt with factors such as attaining jobs, avoiding dependency, being successful and upwardly mobile in different ways. Certain ethnic groups became, because of cultural prerequisites, more likely to be successful in America. Other groups such as blacks and Puerto Ricans exhibited "cultural deprivation" that predisposed them to ongoing poverty (Glazer & Moynihan).

An emphasis upon the psychological roots of poverty led to even greater interests in the acquisition of large numbers of professionally trained social workers in the welfare system. The various training programs were looked upon as a means of establishing ways of preventing ongoing dependency (Buell, pp. 861–891).

This latter aspect of the law allowed for two groups of welfare workers, those who dealt strictly with legal requirements for eligibility for assistance and other bureaucratic demands and "service" workers. These service workers were those skilled in casework psychotherapy. The caseworkers would no longer be burdened with mundane office tasks and could devote themselves to the more creative tasks of psychotherapy involved in the casework relationship. In the long run, these activities were seen as having a potential for decreasing the size of the welfare roles.

Following the assassination of Kennedy, President Johnson introduced the War on Poverty where the elimination of poverty became a top national priority. Social casework now claimed to have the therapeutic means for dealing with rehabilitation of the poor and in the long-run curing people of poverty. The profession again seemed in tune with the national concerns of the time, as it had been in the 1930s. The general feeling was that the profession was again on the brink of assuming leadership in facing national problems.

This social work leadership in professional control of resources was not to be. In the late 1930s, the conservatives opposed social welfare programs. However, this group was seen as causing the problem of the Depression and their opposition had little impact upon the growth of the welfare state. During the 1960s, the programs were attacked not only by the right wing, but also by a large percentage of the middle income population who had reaped the benefits of the expanding economy. They continued to view the poor as an alien and degenerate part of society, unwilling to work and unworthy of assistance. Most importantly, there also grew an increasing discontent with social workers from the poor themselves. Anger was expressed by them about their domination by professional middle class groups and liberals in general. More and more they viewed these professional people as self-serving and engaged in the practice that was at best irrelevant to their problems, and, at worst, a subtle means of oppression that was an alternative to direct coercion.

An early critic of these liberal programs voiced what was to become the theme of the ultimate attack upon casework (Alinsky). Liberal programs, it was said, had failed to meet the needs of the poor. What was required was radical organization or people's organizations of local groups that would have access to resources and power and apply these resources to the needs of the community as the community defined them. Radical community action, not adjustment, was what was called for and social workers and their ilk did not encourage that kind of action:

> They pride themselves on their techniques and talents for adjusting people to difficult situations. They come to the people of the slums under the aegis of benevolence and goodness, not to organize the people, not to help them rebel and fight their way out of the muck—no! They come to get these people "adjusted": adjusted so they will live in hell and like it too. It would be difficult to conceive a higher form of social treason—yet this infamy is perpetrated in the name of charity. Is it any wonder that the men of the slum snarl, "damn your charity. We want jobs."
>
> . . . because the community council can not and does not want to get down to the roots of the problems, it retreats into a sphere of trivial,

superficial ameliorations. The people judge the agency by its program
and soon define the agency as insignificant (Ibid., p. 59).

As the civil rights movement moved to a more assertive stance during the 1960s, the social programs came under more intense attack.
Rather than being simply considered inept or incompetent, programs
and workers were looked upon as agents of a colonial government with
the ghetto being considered a colony of the broader society (Blauner,
p. 87). It was also suggested that programs tended to be mechanisms
for the control of the poor, providing resources to forestall revolution
and withholding these same resources when revolution was no longer a
problem and source of cheap labor was required (Piven & Cloward,
pp. xii-xiv).

There were other less radical positions (Pearl & Riessman). The
professionals, including social workers, were perceived in their work as
unable to understand the full impact of the problems of the poor. The
professional's middle class orientation presented not only a cultural
gap, but also a knowledge gap insofar as survival in a poor neighborhood was concerned. Moreover, casework was viewed as not appropriate to helping the poor in most cases because it did not address itself to
their real problems (Reissman, p. 75).

The poor themselves were said to have certain skills that were miss-
ing in the professionals. Because of a common culture and similar life
experiences, they were better able to understand and communicate
with one another. It was suggested that they be employed to supple-
ment the professionals' activities by bridging the gap between the
client and the helper. This would not only enhance service, but would
make available a vast number of meaningful jobs to the poor. Social
workers and other professional types would be useful as consultants
and trainers provided they retrained themselves so that their skills
would be relevant to the problems that the poor felt they had (Pearl &
Reissman, pp. 220–221). Aides in social work and education became part
of the programs of many agencies and schools as a result of this approach.[1]

In general, acceptance of the new careers idea promoted the notion
of the limits of professionals, particularly those in social work. In the

---

1. In addition to rejecting professionalism, Riessman rejects Alinsky's approach. He states that this manner of dealing with poverty fails in its purpose
wherever it is tried. The basic supposition of Alinsky that the poor desire
power and resources is incorrect. What the poor require, according to Reissman, are jobs. (Reissman, pp. 3–15).

end, social workers, some of them grudgingly, agreed to accept new career people. However, there was a maintenance of sharp salary and status difference in the institutions where they were employed.

In the poverty program *per se*, social workers played only a limited role. In 1965, Congressman Adam Clayton Powell condemned the lack of participation of the poor in local poverty programs. Rather than professionals, poor people needed to be planning the local projects. Powell wanted to stop local Offices of Economic Opportunity from becoming "giant fiestas of political patronage." Some degree of local control was indeed established with programs focusing upon indigenous administration and self-help personnel for the poor (Sundquist, p. 166).

The national interest in social problems in the early 1960s made it seem, at first, that social work would again emerge as a respected profession. Its expertise would be useful in the development and administration of programs to end poverty. But the expertise in social reform was merely a public relations shadow. Social workers were therapists, they were trained in casework and did not have the skills to address the global problems of the times. When they attempted to involve themselves in social reform they often were clumsy, incompetent and sometimes disparaged their clients.

The casework model carried with it attitudes about the poor that widened the gap between the client and the social workers. Troubled people were seen as partially responsible for their problems. Notions such as the "culture of poverty" or "cultural deprivation" were accepted by social workers as they approached the poor. These ideas were viewed by the clients as insulting and prejudiced. At a time when such groups were asserting their pride, they held intense antipathy for those whose ideas suggested that they were inferior.

Finally, considerable concern was raised about the ability of social workers to be helpful even when they applied their casework in appropriate situations. Serious questions came, not only from the poor, but from within the profession as to whether casework accomplished anything at all.

The Effectiveness of Casework

During this time, in dealing with reform, the conservative social workers again constantly gave verbal support to the concept but claimed that general reform was too broad an issue for the profession to tackle. The study and application of sociology was said not to allow for the development of techniques that could be immediately applied to aid the client. Even functioning to bring resources within the grasp of the client or to act as an advocate in a confrontation was looked upon as inappropriate by many therapeutic caseworkers. The client would be robbed of his/her right to choose. One might encourage dependency. There would be a loss of self respect, resentment and a sense of failure about not being allowed to solve one's own problem. The caseworker was to provide the relationship that would enable the client to express emotions and develop insights. These insights would then help the clients to solve their own problems. Direct treatment was defined as "The influence of mind upon mind." (Hollis, pp. 63–69). True help was helping the client to help himself, a "renunciation of 'doing to' and for 'doing with' . . . ." (Simon, p. 378). In short, direct face-to-face therapeutic service was the treatment of choice because it was said to work better, that is, it was more effective and had a more permanent positive effect than environmental manipulation.

By 1960 very little beyond the psychologically oriented casework approach was being taught. Even social group work which had its roots in the recreation and the Deweyan life space education practice in the settlement houses became oriented to therapeutic rehabilitative endeavor.

With such a thorough commitment to the therapeutic model, it was not surprising that social work was severely shaken by questions raised by the purpose and effectiveness of the whole psychiatric establishment beginning in the 1960s. Szaz suggested that psychiatry, rather than a method of helping a client, was simply part of society's control apparatus. Its purpose was to single out and punish wrongdoers (Szaz). Soon, study after study was demonstrating that psychiatric intervention did not seem to ever reach its declared goals.

One study, for example, demonstrated that community mental health programs have little or no effect in the reduction of admissions to state mental hospitals, their self defined goals. Furthermore, these centers seemed to have no accountability to their funding sources, the National Institute of Mental Health, to say nothing of accountability to their clients (Chu & Trotter, pp. xiii–xiv).

Like the mental health centers, professional social work continued to function over the years without accountability. The validity of casework was assumed and demonstrated only through clinical evidence in anecdotal fashion. When any kind of statistical analysis was applied, no determinable effect could be demonstrated. A landmark study reviewed over 70 earlier studies of casework effectiveness conducted between the 1930s and 1972 (Fischer, pp. 5–20). It found that in the studies with experimental and control groups improvement in casework-treated client could not be demonstrated. In fact, in almost half the studies, casework-treated subjects deteriorated or made slower progress than people who received no casework treatment. The conclusion of the study read:

> . . . this review of the available control research strongly suggests that, at present, lack of evidence of the effectiveness of professional casework is the rule rather than the exception. A technical corollary to this conclusion, and a comment frequently appearing in the social work literature is that 'we also lack good scientific proof of ineffectiveness.' This assertion, however, taken alone, would appear to be rather insubstantial grounds on which to support a profession (Ibid., p. 19).

The major reason given for the rejection of social reform in the history of social work was that casework offered an avenue for effective helping. The global nature of social problems and the lack of specific techniques for tackling them made the statement of goals difficult if not impossible. The field therefore needed to concentrate its efforts on the smaller, more manageable problems to get results. The field devoted itself almost entirely to the study of methods that were almost exclusivey psychotherapeutic.

As the poverty program developed, the poor were the first to question the value of such treatment as useful in the solutions of their problems. They were supported by social work researchers whose work seemed to indicate that there was no demonstrable statistical evidence that casework was of any value in reaching its goals. The profession now faced two problems. On the one hand, they were unable to address social problems because they had devoted themselves to the study of psychotherapeutic methods. On the other hand, these methods were being shown to be of little or no use to clients.

There were a variety of ways in which various groups in social work responded to these criticisms. Again, little occurred that moved the profession into substantive areas of creating social change. In fact, professionals seemed to seize upon the opportunity to return to their traditional roles as rehabilitative therapists and protect these roles through denigration of reform and the construction of theories which disguised the actual functioning of the profession.

The Response of Professional Social Work to the Criticism of the 1960s and 1970s

The field faced criticism from radicals and minorities who regarded it as competition for resources. The techniques of casework were seen as irrelevant to the culture or realities of the life of the poor. Other voices within the profession were being raised to question the relevance of casework to any client, poor, wealthy, or middle class. Beyond these people there lurked the political right wing which had opposed social programs from the very beginning, and now blamed social workers for having made them a reality. Their perception of social workers was as ineffectual "bleeding hearts," concerning themselves with undesirables. Because of them, lazy people expected to be catered to and cared for by government, and criminals were not properly punished for the most heinous of crimes. People were paying taxes and social workers were wasting the money. The esteem enjoyed by the profession during the 1930s and 1940s and briefly during the 1960s turned into disdain. In the public's eye, social work and the welfare state were one. The campaign waged against social programs needed scapegoats and social workers were cast in that role. By the early 1970s the profession had few allies anywhere in the American political spectrum. Within the profession a general malaise, depression and acceptance of the negative image of social work seemed to develop (Richan & Mendelsohn). Various strategies were to be developed to maintain the existence of the profession.

The Casework Response

Caseworkers moved swiftly to deal with the criticism. The goal of casework was therapeutic curing. How it was done did not change its goal or philosophic orientation. A variety of therapeutic approaches were tried among different social workers in different areas. Gestalt therapy, Transactional Analysis, even massage was tried by some social workers. Two approaches seemed to have emerged and developed some broadly-based support to retain their pre-eminence and legitimacy within the profession: the "systems approach" and "socio-behavioral practice."

The systems approach involved viewing the client operating in a variety of systems within his/her lifespace or ecology:

> Within the ecological perspective, human beings are conceived as evolving and adapting through transactions with all elements of their environments. In these adaptive processes, the human being and the environment shape each other. People mold their environments in many ways, and in turn, must then adapt to changes they create (Compton & Galaway, p. 29).

Social work is viewed as a method of analyzing the various systems and their interfaces, and intervening where the most improvement for the client can be accomplished. One may address macro systems (communities, groups, etc.) or microsystems (individuals or couples) with the understanding that problems have multiple causality and can be worked in a variety of ways:

> Social work's distinctive functions and tasks arise from its social purpose: to strengthen patterns of people and to improve environments so that a better match can be obtained between people's adaptive needs and potential and the qualities of their impinging environment. Professional action is directed toward helping people in their environments overcome obstacles that inhibit the development of adaptive capacities (Ibid.).

A technology incorporating interaction and social functioning suggested by the systems framework did not emerge. What seemed to develop from this model was a theoretical framework that enabled the incorporation of the existing methodologies. This approach does not deny the legitimacy of social reform. It is considered a level of intervention. However, such intervention, when it is illustrated, usually is in the area which we have earlier defined as Mary Richmond's retail reform, i.e., the bringing together of resources to ameliorate problems in specific cases (Pincus & Minahan, pp. 289–308). Activism and direct intervention in political matters are not denied. They are simply ignored.

In the main, the systems approach is not (Cloward & Piven, p. 58) an attractive one for those interested in functional methodological or social change. What it introduces into the profession is a new vocabulary, massive, often incomprehensible, and sometimes mystical. It has been used to provide a place for the practice of existing therapeutic techniques and makes little demand upon them for change or accountability. In the end, it is a life-space refuge where professionals can ply their existing trade in familiar ecological niches protected by the armor of massive jargon. Its practical value remains to be unlocked with the development of a technology that makes general use of an interaction of systems.

The socio-behavioral approach offered casework more substance. Recognizing the problem of the lack of effectiveness in casework from the beginning, it incorporated certain elements of the psychology known as behaviorism that spoke directly to the accomplishment of predefined goals.

Socio-behavioral practice bases its perspective upon the application of information that is the product of empirical research. Every applied approach in socio-behavioral practice has been documented to a greater or lesser extent to be effective in a given situation through empirical research (Thomas, pp. 181–218). The hallmark of the approach is a clear-cut, accurate, and specific definition of every facet of the therapeutic endeavor. Careful definition of goals, contract and progress are part of every casework encounter. The client is taken through various steps in the casework relationship. The problem must be observable and is identified in specific rather than global terms. It becomes the target and a baseline goal is established again in measureable and observable terms. A specific behavioral technique is applied and the direction of change is measured throughout the course of treatment. The outcome is also measured, thus giving an account of the effectiveness of the treatment for each client. Finally, there is even a provision for the maintenance of change and measurement within this particular method of practice.

Socio-behavioral casework consists of a variety of empirically determined techniques bound together in what is called "Effective Casework Practice." There has been only a limited acceptance of such practice by professionals. Instead, a variety of criticisms have been leveled against socio-behavioral practice. The criticisms fall into two broad categories, one having to do with behaviorism as manipulative mind control and the other dealing with the required specificity as dehumanizing and reducing the client's problem to meaningless but manageable dimensions.

Mind control and the application of psychology to control behavior has long been grist for science fiction. This "Clockwork Orange" myth, while representing a half-truth, is no more true of behaviorism than any other means of dealing with human functioning. There are many ways of manipulating human behavior. The application of non-behavioral techniques of manipulation in case work have been amply demonstrated in this study. Behaviorism makes no bones about its purpose and is for that reason perhaps more vulnerable to attack. However, unlike other methods of control, the behavioral approach, when ethically applied, delineates the dimensions of the target, the methods and goals clearly and concisely. There must be full understanding of the process by all concerned. When practiced in a non-institutional setting, socio-behavioral casework can allow for a greater degree of client participation in the entire therapeutic process than any other method. The client can be intimately involved in the identification of the problem, the method of therapy and choice of that therapy, and the ultimate goals of therapy. What occurs is thoroughly defined, clearly understandable; and often there is a written contract between client and therapist (Gambrill, Thomas and Carter, p. 61).

The argument that behaviorism suffers because of its reductionism has a bit more substance. In its efforts to make its content clear and accurate, behaviorism can justifiably be accused of robbing life of some of its substance. However, this objection is often melodramatically overstated:

> . . . most psychological theorists treat human beings as superior robots, responding to environmental stimulae. This is most obvious in behavioral theory, which treats humans as though they were rats, not live rats, but ones that have been robbed of all their natural individuality by statistical averaging (Compton & Galloway, pp. 100–101).

Such criticism reflects a stereotype rather than knowledge of sociobehavioral practice. The field has developed techniques and applications far more complex than those implied by such critics at the present time. Concepts within behaviorism such as contracting, understandable goal setting, and client involvement in planning have had application and wide acceptance beyond practice in the socio-behavioral areas.

In the end behaviorism does effect change in the areas it defines as problems and can demonstrate it. It is problematical whether other theories in any way provide a service that is so demonstrably effective in any area. To the behaviorist, sloppy, nebulous definition served the philosophical idealism of the therapist, not the needs of the client.

The narrowness of the behaviorist approach does lend legitimacy to the argument that it devotes its entire practice effort to changing the individual. While in no way does the theory oppose or minimize social action, it also does not encourage it. The environment, except for the directly involved stimulae, is usually ignored. Even at its best, then, it addresses itself to a small facet of human difficulties. In terms of the perceived problems of many of the people served by social workers that psychological element is basically only a minor portion of their difficulties.

Social work entered the 1960s as a profession that had completely devoted itself to a helping model based upon psychotherapy. When the nation began to concern itself with poverty it turned to social work in the hope that the expertise that had characterized the New Deal social workers would again be available to ameliorate the problems being addressed. The psychotherapeutically oriented caseworkers were not up to the task. The New Dealers had been absorbed into government and there was no young group with fresh ideas to replace them.

Their lack of skills in reform caused those social workers who attempted to become involved in social change to bungle badly. Not only were they without the necessary training for the task but they were beset with a theory base that insulted and denigrated their clients. These workers were accused of blaming the victims of poverty, regarding their clients as inferior human beings and competing for the limited resources available to help the poor. When they attempted to apply casework, the social workers found that they were regarded as concerning themselves with irrelevant problems by the poor. Therapy was not required to deal with poverty, according to the poor, it was social reform, jobs, and fair distribution of resources that was needed.

To respond to this need activist community organizations experienced a rebirth in the 1960s. They began to approach reform issues. The value and success of this method of practice was also questioned and it too needed to deal with its critics.

The Response of the Organizers

The 1960s caused an upheaval in the perceptions that the organizers had of themselves. The call to more direct action by Alinsky (Alinsky) was first made in 1949 but not heard until the 1960s. It demanded that organizers address themselves to relevant issues—more specifically, the full gamut of responses to problems needed to be made by all manner of social workers, including advocacy where clients had been wronged (N.A.S.W. Ad Hoc Committee on Advocacy, pp. 16–22). Organizers could no longer satisfy themselves by raising funds or breaking down communication barriers between people when they shared the same goals and needed to join forces to take action against a common problem. There was conflict in the real world. The clients of social workers were often disadvantaged in such conflicts. They frequently lacked resources and organizations and were overwhelmed by the powerful forces that opposed them.

The expertise of community organization social workers needed to be brought to bear upon the situation. It was legitimate for the profession to act to even the balance a bit. Skills, such as the ability to bargain, politically manipulate and even employ tactics of direct confrontation need not be off-limits to the professional (Brager & Specht, pp. 253–254). Community organization was said to have different specializations that accounted for the different legitimate activities that fell within its sphere. "Locality development" involved bringing together elements within a community to achieve common goals. "Social planning" dealt with a technical process of problem solving including fund raising and grant writing. Finally, "social action" was the community organization process that should be applied in a situation of conflict (Rothman, pp. 20–36).

The pressure from the minorities that followed on the heels of the poverty program, questioning the right and effectiveness of the social work organizers to be involved in the program per se, frustrated the organizers. In addition, social work organization received more and more opposition from the political right which had gained strength after the election of Richard Nixon as President and conservative governors like James Rhodes of Ohio and Ronald Reagan of California. The profession, already shaken by attacks against casework soon seemed anxious to divest itself of the reform role. This position is clearly stated in a review of a book with an activist approach to social work practice:

> A basic assumption of the book is that social work is inherently political, which confuses the term political with ideas of power and status; and makes for a rejection of the public political process. It is a pernicious idea that has cost social workers dearly in recent years. Galper's rejection of the contractual relations of social workers with society, employing agencies, and clients reveals an elitist orientation that seeks to exploit powerless clients for which may be alien political processes. Social work currently needs new, relevant strategies that are not "radical," or "political," in posture. It can profit from the lessons of recent events to formulate a realistic revitalized professional paradigm of practice that can better help achieve the profession's purposes of social change, regain public support, and provide more effective forms of helping practice (Siporin, p. 520).

This criticism of activism began early in the 1960s. In addition to the fears of loss of support, emphasis was placed upon the powerlessness of social work and futility of action that might in the long run be destructive to the profession. Gradually those involved in social action turned their backs on any involvement and again began to support their safer, more traditional roles.

A leading community organization specialist gives a stunning example of the field's turn-about. In 1969 Specht spoke about the legitimacy of disruptive tactics in situations of social conflict (pp. 5–15). While he eschews direct personal involvement in violence and differentiates between disruption and insurrection, he sees a social work role in all of these areas. In such conflicts social workers can operate in, for example, negotiations and bargaining as expert advocates. Most importantly, he does not urge or encourage the professional to oppose conflict per se which was the traditional posture:

When community issues are perceived by one group as eliminating or diminishing its power over others, the result will be dissensus; contest and disruption. To carve a place out for itself in the political social order, a new group may have to fight for a reorientation of many of the values of the older order. . . . in these kinds of change efforts . . . the role of the community workers is that of partisan or organizer (Ibid.).

A short time later an article by the same author blames activism and identification with Marxism as responsible for the destruction of the professional character of social work (Specht, 1972, pp. 3–15). He sees the results of such activity by social workers as resulting in the universal disenchantment with social work:

Who has anything positive to say about professional social workers? Clients? Certainly not the mainstay of social work—the poor and the minorities. Government? Not likely. Once a reform era has ended, social workers—who were utilized as bureaucrats during the liberal reform period—are considered in Lubove's phrase "Professional Altruists," who serve government as ineffectual consciences—in residence. As care-takers for the lame and the blind, they also serve as important social function, always well-meaning and at times appreciated for their development of an ideology and set of practical skills geared to the amelioration of human suffering. More recently, however, many professional altruists have become political activists, and this is a transformation the government will neither accept nor forgive. Whom does that leave? The Blue and White collar workers and the hard hats of middle America do not think the profession offers any benefit to them and probably perceive they are held in contempt by its more militant and outspoken members (Ibid.)

The reactions seem to reflect the desire to engage in genuine social change even in the presence of conflict and yet also the feelings of being ineffectual, beaten, and afraid of the risk.

Professional education itself seemed to continue mired in traditional casework practice. Early in the 1960s, as reform again became legitimate, the schools began to recognize some of their kinship to the New Deal program. One aspect of the change was the utilization of public assistance and other "atypical" agencies as field placements. Agencies could be host to independent field units supervised and administered by faculty who made use of the agency caseloads. Schools could also set up service centers that were separate agencies coordinating the number of community agencies including public assistance agencies as well as the new agencies functioning in the poverty program.

Social work schools, however, were slow to respond to methodological changes. Students were uncomfortable with this lack of responsiveness. They sought to participate in a school governance process that delineated the content of professional training. Most importantly, they pressed for content that could provide insight into ways of coping with problems of society and its effect upon their clients. Casework approaches seemed woefully inadequate (Erlich & Tropman, 1974, pp. 22–26).

Although the schools introduced some courses and piecemeal material in the social action areas pressed for by students, the main thrust of education still remained in treating the individual. The introduction of protective theoretical frameworks such as systems theory has been the most lasting outcome of the response to the student movement. The withdrawal of the professional organizers from social action has spread apparently to the student body. Recent studies document students' preoccupation with grades, lack of interest in activism, and even passive and active support for the current anti-welfare positions of political conservatives (Miller, pp. 268–271; Blum & Rosenberg, 524–525). The view clearly has developed that social work's political involvement has resulted in the decline of the profession.

Summary

After the war, the liberals and other less radical social workers abandoned social reform stances that would jeopardize their employment. The field became almost totally involved in the less controversial practice advocated by the caseworkers. The mainstream of social work returned to the psychotherapeutic-counseling method that characterized the profession before the New Deal.

When the government tried to address poverty and other social problems in the 1960s, social workers again attempted to devise and administer programs. This time they failed miserably. Casework training had not prepared them for the role of social reformer. Instead, many of the premises of the method alienated them from their clients. Social workers were rejected by the poor as insensitive to the issues of their clients, offering little or no competency or expertise in needed skills and engaging in a so-called helping process, namely casework, that had nothing to do with the problems under consideration.

Criticism about the effectiveness and usefulness of casework began to be heard from another quarter. The researchers had accumulated evidence that casework was statistically of questionable value. They proposed that the field modify practice so that it could demonstrate its effectiveness.

Only one fragment of the profession responded by adapting the techniques of behavioral psychology and social psychology to social work practice. The remainder became defensive and either ignored the critics or sought refuge in a newly developed organizing framework taken from systems analysis. This approach seems to have offered no substantive change in casework practice. Rather it encased existing practices in jargon and theoretical obfuscation that made criticism more difficult. This was not unlike the incorporation of the psychiatric model that had occurred earlier in the profession's history. The end result of this process is a beleaguered and battle-weary profession. It has returned to the casework model in the hope that this will preserve a niche for it amongst America's professions.

Chapter 9

Social Work Today:
Current Trends and Conclusions

Radical critiques of social work have found its history a chronicle of failure to deliver services and meet its goals, particularly as they relate to poor and minority populations. They see the cause of this as the inability of the profession to function outside of the framework of the capitalist system. This system, it is claimed, has been designed by the priviledged to meet their own needs and preserve their status. Programs that seem to assist others are a sham, Potempkin's villages, that disguise the true nature of their insidious purpose. Hidden within each program is a system of mechanisms that prevent services and resources from reaching target populations and ultimately cause the failure of the programs themselves. The true purpose of such programs is the preservation of the existing structure and system while giving the appearance of promoting change. This explains social work's failure at social reform. Activism, to be truly successful, must support the destruction of the current system and the establishment of a new and equitable order through violent and/or non-violent revolution (Galper, pp. 175–176).

While this argument has appealed to a very few, the vast majority of practicing social workers find it an unsatisfactory solution to social problems. As our history has shown, social workers are generally not revolutionary by inclination or by training. They are often middle-class women with college educations and usually a genuine desire to be helpful to people who are having difficulty. There are many instances of courageous efforts by social workers on their clients' behalf. Nonetheless, this courage has rarely been extended to fomenting, encouraging or participating in revolution for a variety of reasons.

The most pervasive of these reasons is that social workers, like many others, question the effectiveness of revolution. Revolutions produce their own stratification and special interests that use the structure of the government to protect their own interests just as their predecessors did. Furthermore, revolution is the most risky, dangerous and destructive of change strategies for both the perpetrators and their followers. Most importantly, their clients, the supposed beneficiaries of such action, share in the distaste for moving in that direction.

Finding an agency position that offers revolution with job security is also a challenge. Social workers are employment-oriented and while they are genuinely committed toward helping their clients, they are also inclined to want to do so while earning a living. Since activism has been tied to revolutionary rhetoric, the only alternative that seems to be left to them is helping through apolitical psychotherapeutic casework or groupwork. Activism as revolution is seen as outside of effective and appropriate professional functioning. Attacking liberal practice as useless and hopeless, as some radicals have (Ibid., pp. 1–4), has not encouraged interest in social reform. Rather, it has encouraged defensiveness and has alienated the reformers from the rest of the profession.

The fact remains that the profession has engaged in non-revolutionary activism throughout its history. The answer to the question of whether it has been successful is dependent upon the definition of success. If it is defined as creating a permanent order that can not be unraveled then it has indeed been a failure. However, that is a grandiose measure of success. In the last analysis, social work has taken successful action for the improvement of American life by developing and sponsoring social programs that have enjoyed widespread acceptance and support from government and throughout the population. While the programs have been demonstrated to be limited in terms of reaching their goals of eliminating such social problems as poverty, they have also had some measure of success. The pain that retrenchment has caused to the populations served by the programs is witness to that.

In casework with individuals the profession has begun to respond to the call for effective practice (Reid & Hanrahan, pp. 328–340). Although many practitioners doggedly cling to timeworn psychodynamic practice, sociobehavioral practice is beginning to have some impact upon the field. There has been a framework for the application of systems theory beyond mystification (Pincus & Minahan). A much needed technology for the application of this framework is developing through problem solving casework and methods of discovering and making use of social networks.

The profession has not been totally inactive in the political arena.

Three current members of congress were social workers before running for office and strongly support the programs and ideals of the profession. The National Association of Social Workers functions through a political action committee to lobby for programs supportive of the profession and of benefit to its clients. In a variety of agency settings as practitioners and board members social workers have continued to promote programs supporting planned parenthood, civil rights issues for minorities and women, and services for the disabled.

These efforts, however, represent only a fraction of the functioning in the profession. The mainstream of social workers have reacted in ways that have become its unfortunate tradition. The field has become defensive and self protective. A recent study of the members of the National Association of Social Workers reported that between 1972 and 1982 there has been an increase of over ten percent of social workers in the area of mental health (N.A.S.W., pp. 7–9). This aspect of social work represents well over a third of the employment of N.A.S.W. members. Other categories such as "family work" indicate that still more of the profession is engaged in psychotherapeutically oriented casework. The sharpest decline during the ten-year period occurred in the public assistance arena. Current employment in this area is now just over one percent. Another decline was in community organization where the number of employed N.A.S.W. members is well below one percent. While some of this drop can be attributed to cutbacks, it also is fair to assume that some has resulted from the voluntary movement of practitioners out of these fields.

Education in social work has taken on an ominous turn. For a number of years there has been training in the variety of modes of practice at all levels of intervention. Students would choose to specialize in a variety of concentrations in such areas as mental health, child welfare, services to the aged, corrections and services to the poor. There has been a greater and greater interest in the mental health arena with the belief that it is here where the jobs will be found. The schools have responded with a continued apparent interest in the concentration of specialization ideas. However, within the curriculum, a great deal of emphasis is now being placed upon the dilution of this content. It has been assumed that the most effective practitioners will be those who can function at a variety of levels within the lifespace of the client. It is being proposed that considerable time during graduate training be spent in training "generalist" social workers (Anderson, pp. 37–45). There is a rebirth of the interest of finding "common" content applicable in all social work, a so-called "generic" curriculum that would provide a base for all practice. As we have seen, both notions have their historical counterpart where the end result has almost always been exclusive emphasis upon individual direct practice. This result is from casework becoming defined as the common denominator of social work. It is reasonable to assume that this will again become the trend, particularly if retrenchment in funding continues and the job market is perceived to be in psychotherapeutic areas.

Predictions about the social work job market are notoriously difficult to make. The social policy of federal and state governments are the major variables. Current layoffs have cut across the entire field. Decreases in funding have reduced the availability of funds for vendor payments, affecting the income of private practitioners in casework. In addition, there have been increased employment opportunities in social work in health and child welfare, although on a more modest plane than in mental health. A shift toward the mental health perspective could be interpreted as not so much a reflection of the job market, but of the personal preferences of the social work leadership.

The current social welfare and education policies are often perceived as a reflection of the cyclical nature of American government. They are at variance with the past fifty years of development in that area. In addition, there are predictions of serious economic difficulties growing out of gargantuan governmental deficits, the inability of foreign countries to pay their debts, and predicted increases in interest rates and unemployment. Such a crisis and turnabout in policy could again require the creative minds of skilled practitioners to develop, implement and administer programs that would address social problems. In the 1960s we faced just such a crisis with little to offer but caseworkers trained in individual practice. Educational programs in organization, planning and administration came too late to provide the leadership that came from the settlement houses in the 1930s. If we again abandon social activism as a major component of social work practice we will again be unable to meet the needs of the coming challenge in social reform. The field need not abandon a commitment to casework. It must, however, also not abandon a commitment to address the social problems that plague the clients it serves.

The preoccupation with the job market presents another pitfall. There is the inclination of social workers to move the total focus of the profession wherever there is the slightest hint of available funds. This reactive posture puts us in the position of supporting the political motives of those whose purpose might be at variance with the objectives of our profession. Furthermore, frequent shifts in political strategies place social work in the position of having concentrated our energies in yesterday's issues and consistently needing to redirect our attention to the current vogue. During the election year of 1984 we are seeing the Reagan administration seeking to minimize its image as destroyers of social programs. Thus there has been renewed expressed interest in certain social issues that will contrast with the decimation of services in the preceeding years of the administration. The areas chosen include school discipline, substance abuse and physical and sexual abuse of children. Social work seems to have entered full tilt in supporting the move for services for abused children.

It goes without saying that social work's traditional interest in helping victimized children remains an important commitment for the profession. However, our full partnership with the current administration must be approached very gingerly. The profession must be aware of the political motives behind the funding and the possibility of the interest ·in service being short lived. We must also be cognizant of the effects of activities social workers are being asked to perform in the interest of ameliorating child abuse. Early detection of potential child abusers, for example, poses the danger of applying invalid and unreliable measures to clients whose lives could be irrepairably damaged by being falsely accused. The outcome could again place social workers in the role of oppressive social control agents, alienating our clients and others who support them. The ultimate failure of such a detection program could also be used to discredit the profession to the general population. This would not be unlike the damage the profession suffered because of its involvement in the War on Poverty.

What must guide professional social work in defining the direction of practice is a clear definition of its purpose and ideology. Our activities must reflect the pursuit of carefully delineated and consistent goals. In every instance we must be aware that each activity and every choice that the profession makes has ideological and political implications. As we have seen again and again in our material, choices about programs, methodology, standards for professional performance and theoretical framework do not occur in a vacuum. The face of contemporary social work has been determined by actions in these very areas. Social work education must help professionals to develop a sensitivity to the full range of possible impact of such decision making.

What is particularly required is sophistication of social work practitioners about theory, albeit contrary to the teaching of Mary Richmond and her followers in the contemporary leadership of social work. The awareness of the profession that no choice can be made without an ideological implication must extend to our understanding of the theoretical foundations of the profession. We have chosen to apply the medical model, psychiatric and developmental and other psychological theory as our predominant base. Yet, we pay little attention to the implications of the application of these theories upon our practice.

Both the medical model and psychiatric theory treat clients as patients who need to be diagnosed and treated so that they will be cured of an illness. The attitude of the practitioner about role definition and his or her view of the client are clearly shaped by such a perspective. Psychological theory defines problems as intrapsychic or learned and unlearned and attacks problem solving from these perspectives. Developmental theory looks for the roots of problems in the client's history and deals with helping in terms of insight into past events. Too often professionals have chosen one orientation or another using apparent pragmatic justification but in ignorance of how the application impacts upon the client or clients and the social worker.

Through the history of social work we have shown a recurring call for a particular theoretical orientation, applied social science or sociology. For a variety of reasons—political, professional and ideological—this call has been largely ignored. Yet such a theory base offers a sound basis for the understanding of human functioning taking into account the full spectrum of factors that determine behavior. It provides an understanding of the effect of interaction between individuals and institutions. Most importantly, it provides a picture of the client as a functioning agent within a realistic environment acting and being acted upon. A technology based upon such a theory need not assume illness, wrongdoing or deviant functioning *a priori* but can proceed to intervene in a variety of levels to ameliorate difficulties. It would seem that such a technology stressing interaction would be called for within the context of the popular systems approach to social work.

This sociological-anthropological approach provides a wealth of information at both micro-systems and macro-systems levels. The interaction of individuals and its behavioral impact is the subject of the seminal works of Erving Goffman (see for example 1959, 1963, & 1974) and the ethnomethodologists (Grinnell, pp. 361–372). Here the actions of people who face stigmatization and other difficulties are viewed within the context of their victimization and their response to it. The use of such theory could produce a technology that would blunt the pain of stigma and promote the sharing of mechanisms that assist people in dealing with their perception of themselves as discredited. Other areas that provide enormous potential for practice but have enjoyed, at most, very limited application to practice are notions of exchange in social settings, the impact and development of norms and role theory.

At higher levels of intervention there exists a plethora of information about social stratification, culture and political functioning that are often talked about but seldom applied in practice. This theoretical information provides a wealth of potential in reform activities as well as administrative and planning activities.

The argument has been frequently made about the applicability of such social science epistomology and practice. Instead of using this social science, social work has opted to use psychological theory because of the existence of a technology in spite of its apparent negative ideological impact. Social science theory still has drawbacks with regard to its direct applicability. While there have been few successful efforts in the development of a technology, the fact remains that the theory provides content that relates to the broad range of behavior without the negative impact upon the ideology of practice that seems a part of the exclusive use of existing psychological practice. The profession needs to consider a fuller understanding of this information with an eye toward the development of a methodology that will permit broader use by practitioners.

In summary, we have considered the alternatives for the future of social work. Practice within the existing structure of social programs and its radical alternative have been considered. It has been suggested that successful activist practice remains a possibility within the current system as it was during the 1930s. The profession, to accomplish this, must become involved in certain activities. These include an understanding of the implications of professional decisions, sophistication about the theoretical foundation of practice and the application of the untapped wealth of theoretical material available in social science as a new theory base for the profession.

Bibliography

BOOKS

Abbott, Edith. 1942. *Social Welfare and Professional Education.* Chicago: University of Chicago Press.

Addams, Jane. 1893. *Philanthropy and Social Progress.* New York: Thomas Crowell and Company.

————. 1910. *Twenty Years at Hull House.* New York: MacMillan Company.

Alinsky, Saul D. 1946. *Reville for Radicals.* New York: Random House (Vintage Edition, 1969).

American Association of Social Workers. 1929. *Social Case Work, Generic and Specific.* New York: American Association of Social Workers.

American Psychiatric Association. 1980. *Diagnostic Statistical Manual of Mental Disorders.* 3rd edition; Washington, D.C.: American Psychiatric Association.

Bendix, Reinhard. 1960. *Max Weber, An Intellectual Portrait.* Garden City, New York: Doubleday and Company, Inc.

Berengarten, Sidney and Irene H. Kerrigan. 1968. *Interviewing and Personality Assessment: Selection of Social Work Students.* New York: Council on Social Work Education.

Berkowitz, William R. 1982. Community Impact: Creating Grassroots Change in Hard Times. Cambridge, Massachusetts: Schenkman.

Bernard, L. L. and Jessie Bernard. 1943. *Origins of American Sociology.* New York: Thomas Crowell Company.

Bishop, Margaret. 1948. *The Selection and Admission of Students in a School of Social Work.* Philadelphia, Pennsylvania: University of Pennsylvania, School of Social Work.

Blauner, Robert. 1972. *Racial Oppression in America.* New York: Harper and Row.

Brackett, Jeffrey Richardson, 1903. *Supervision and Education in Charity.* New York: The Macmillan Company.

Brager, George and Harry Specht. 1973. *Community Organizing.* New York: Columbia University Press.

Bremner, Robert. 1960. *American Philanthropy.* Chicago: University of Chicago Press.

Bruno, Frank J. 1957. *Trends in Social Work, 1874–1956.* New York: Columbia University Press.

Buell, Bradley and Associates. 1952. *Community Planning for Human Services.* New York: Columbia University Press.

Burghardt, Steve. 1982. *The Other Side of Organizing: Personal Dilemmas in Political Demeanor.* Cambridge, Massachusetts: Schenkman.

Cartwright, Dorwin and A. Zander (eds.) 1968. *Group Dynamics: Research and Theory.* New York: Harper and Row.

Chu, Franklin D. and Charland Trotter (eds.). 1974. *The Madness Establishment: Ralph Nader's Study Group Report on the National Institute of Mental Health.* New York: Grossman Publishers.

Colcord, Joanna C. and Ruth Z. M. Mann (eds.). 1930. *The Long View, Papers and Addresses by Mary E. Richmond.* New York: Russell Sage Foundation.

Compton, Beulah Roberts and Burt Galaway (eds.). 1979. *Social Work Processes.* Homewood, Illinois: The Dorsey Press.

Cox, Fred W., John L. Ehrlich, Jack Rothman, and John Tropman (eds.). 1970. *Strategies of Community Organization.* Itasca, Illinois: F. E. Peacock Publishers.

Davis, Allen F. 1967. *Spearhead for Reform, the Social Settlements and the Progressive Movement, 1880–1914.* New York: Oxford University Press.

Dunham, Arthur. 1970. *The New Community Organization.* New York: Thomas Y. Crowell Co., Inc.

Etzioni, Amitai (ed.). 1969. *The Semi-Professionals and their Organization.* New York: The Free Press.

Faatz, Anita J. 1953. *The Nature of Choice in Casework Process.* Chapell Hill, North Carolina: The University of North Carolina Press.

Fischer, Joel. 1978. *Effective Casework Practice, An Eclectic Approach.* New York: McGraw-Hill.

Fisher, Jacob. 1936. *The Rank and File Movement in Social Work 1931–1936.* New York: New York School of Social Work.

———. 1980. *The Response of Social Work to the Depression.* Cambridge, Massachusetts: Schenkman.

Galper, Jeffery. 1975. *The Politics of Social Services.* Englewood Cliffs, New Jersey: Prentice Hall.

Gil, David. 1982. *Unravelling Social Policy.* Cambridge, Massachusetts: Schenkman.

Glasser, Paul, Rosemary Sarri, and Robert Vinter (eds.). 1974. *Individual Change through Small Groups.* New York: The Free Press.

Glazer, Nathan and Daniel Patrick Moynihan. 1964. *Beyond the Melting Pot.* Cambridge, Massachusetts: The M.I.T. Press.

Goffman, Erving. 1963. *Behavior in Public Places.* New York: The Free Press of Glenco.

———. 1959. *The Presentation of Self in Everyday Life.* Garden City, New York: Doubleday.

———. 1974. *Stigma.* New York: Jason Aronson.

Grinnell, Jr., Robet M. 1981. *Social Work Research and Evaluation.* Itasca, Illinois: F. E. Peacock Publishers, Inc.

Hagarty, James Edward. 1931. The Training of Social Workers. New York: McGraw-Hill Co., Inc.

Halbert, L. A. 1923. *What is Professional Social Work?* New York: The Survey.

Harrington, Michael. 1969. *The Other America: Poverty in the United States.* New York: Macmillan Publishing Company.

Hasenfeld, Yeheshkel and Richard English. 1974. *Human Service Organizations.* Ann Arbor, Michigan. University of Michigan Press.

Hofstadter, Richard. 1955. *Age of Reform.* New York: Random House.

———. 1948. *The American Political Tradition.* New York: Random House Vintage Books.

Hofstadter, Richard and Walter P. Metzger, 1955. *The Development of Academic Freedom in the United States.* New York: Columbia University Press.

Hollis, Ernest V. and Alice L. Taylor. 1951. *Social Work Education in the United States.* New York: Columbia University Press.

Hopkins, Harry. 1972. *Spending to Save.* Seattle, Washington: University of Washington Press.

Jones, Betty Lacey (ed.). 1969, *Current Patterns in Field Instruction in Graduate Social Work Education.* New York: Council on Social Work Education.

Karpf, Maurice J. 1931, *The Scientific Basis of Social Work.* New York: Columbia University Press.

Kolko, Gabriel. 1963. *The Triumph of Conservatism.* New York: Macmillan Publishing Company.

Lasch, Christopher (ed.). 1965. *The Social Thought of Jane Addams.* Indianapolis, Indiana: The Bobbs Merril Company.

Lee, Porter, 1935. "Social Work: Cause and Function." *Proceedings of the Fifty-Sixth Annual Meeting, National Conference of Social Work.* Chicago: University of Chicago Press.

Lee, Porter and Marion E. Kenworthy. 1931. *Mental Hygiene and Social Work.* New York: Commonwealth Press.

Leiby, James. 1978. *A History of Social Welfare and Social Work in the United States.* New York: Columbia University Press.

Lens, Sidney. 1966. *Radicalism in America.* Cambridge, MA, Schenkman Publishing Co.

Levy, Charles S. 1966. *Social Work Education and Practice, 1898–1955.* New York: Wurzwiler School of Social Work, Yeshiva University.

Li, Hong-Chan. 1978. *Social Work Education: A Bibliography.* Metuchen, New Jersey: The Scarecrow Press, Inc.

Lubove, Roy. 1965. *The Professional Altruist.* Cambridge, Massachusetts: Harvard University Press.

Mark, Kenneth L. 1945. *Delayed by Fire; Being the Early History of Simmons College.* (printed privately.)

Mathews, Marie A. 1981. *The Social Work Mystique.* Washington: University Press of America.

Meier, Elizabeth G. 1954. *A History of the New York School of Social Work.* New York: Columbia University Press.

Mills, C. Wright. 1939. *Power, Politics and People.* London: Oxford University Press.

Morison, Samuel Eliot and Henry Steele Commager. 1962. *The Growth of the American Republic.* New York: Oxford University Press.

Pearl, Arthur and Frank Riessman. 1965. *New Careers for the Poor.* New York: The Free Press.

Perkins, Francis. 1946. *The Roosevelt I Knew.* New York: The Viking Press.

Pincus, Alan and Anne Minahan. 1973. *Social Work Practice: Model and Method.* Itasca, Illinois: F. E. Peacock, Publishers.

Piven, Frances Fox and Richard A. Cloward. 1982. *The New Class War.* New York: Pantheon Books.

————. 1971. *Regulating the Poor: The Function of Public Welfare.* New York: Random House.

Platt, Anthony. 1969. *The Child Savers, the Invention of Delinquency.* Chicago: University of Chicago Press.

Pumphery, Ralph E. and Muriel W. Pumphery. 1961. *The Heritage of American Social Work.* New York: Columbia University Press.

Queen, Stuart Alfred. 1922. *Social Work in the Light of History.* Philadelphia: J. B. Lipincott Company.

Reasons, Charles E. and William D. Perdue. 1981. *The Ideology of Social Problems.* Sherman Oaks, California: Alfred Publishing Company.

Reissman, Frank. 1969. *Strategies Against Poverty.* New York: Random House.

Reynolds, Bertha. 1942. *Learning and the Learner in the Practice of Social Work.* New York: Rinehart and Company.

————. 1963. *An Uncharted Journey.* New York: The Citadel Press.

Richan, Willard C. and Allan R. Mendelsohn. 1973. *Social Work, the Unloved Profession.* New York: New Viewpoints.

Richmond, Mary. 1899. *Friendly Visiting Amongst the Poor.* Baltimore, Maryland: Russell Sage Foundation.

————. 1917. *Social Diagnosis.* New York: Russell Sage Foundation.

————. 1922. *What is Social Casework?* New York: Russell Sage Foundation.

Riordon, William L. 1948. *Plunkitt of Tammany Hall.* New York: A. A. Knopf.

Roberts, Robert and Robert Nee (eds.). 1970. *Theories of Social Casework.* Chicago: University of Chicago Press.

Robinson, Virginia. 1930. *A Changing Psychology in Social Case Work.* Chapel Hill, North Carolina: University of North Carolina Press.

Robinson, Virginia (ed.). 1942. *Training for Skill in Social Casework.* Philadelphia, Pennsylvania: University of Pennsylvania Press.

Ross, Murray. 1967. *Community Organization: Theory, Principles and Practice.* New York: Harper and Row.

Rudolph, Frederick. 1962. *The American College and University, A History.* New York: Alfred Knopf Publishing Company.

Schlessinger, Arthur. 1951. *The Rise of Modern America, 1815–1951.* New York: The MacMillan Company.

Schlessinger, Jr., Arthur. 1957. *The Age of Roosevelt, Volume I, The Crisis of the Older Order.* Boston: Houghton-Mifflin Company

Schlessinger, Jr., Arthur. 1959. *The Age of Roosevelt, Volume II, The Coming of the New Deal.* Boston: Houghton-Mifflin Company.

Schlessinger, Jr., Arthur. 1960. *The Age of Roosevelt, Volume III, The Politics of Upheaval.* Boston: Houghton-Mifflin Company.

Sheffield, Ada Eliot. 1937. *Social Insight in Case Situations.* New York: Appleton Century Company.

Siporin, Max. 1975. *Introduction to Social Work Practice.* New York: Macmillan Publishing Company.

Spano, Rick. 1982. *The Rank and File Movement in Social Work.* Washington, D.C.: University Press of America.

Steiner, Jesse Fredrick. 1921. *Education for Social Work.* Chicago: University of Chicago Press.

Study Committee, American Association of Schools of Social Work. 1942. *Education for the Public Social Services.* Chapel Hill, North Carolina: University of North Carolina Press.

Sundquist, James L. (ed.). 1969. *On Fighting Poverty: Perspectives from Experience.* New York: Basic Books.

Szaz, Thomas. 1961.*The Myth of Mental Illness: Foundation of a Theory of Personal Conduct.* New York: Harper and Row.

Thompson, Clara, Milton Mazer, and Earl Whitenberg (eds.). 1955. *An Outline of Psychoanalysis.* New York: The Modern Library, Random House.

Towle, Charlotte. 1945. *Common Human Needs.* Washington, D.C.: United States Government Printing Office.

————. 1954. *The Learner in Education for the Professions as Seen in Education for Social work.* Chicago: University of Chicago Press.

Trattner, Walter. 1974. *From Poor Law to Welfare State.* New York: Free Press.

Tufts, James H. 1923. *Education and Training for Social Work.* New York: Russell Sage Foundation.

Turner, Francis (ed.). 1979. *Social Work Treatment: Interlocking Theoretical Approaches.* Second Edition; New York: The Free Press.

Walker, Sydnor H. 1928. *Social Work and the Training of Social Workers.* Chapel Hill, North Carolina: The University of North Carolina Press.

Weber, Max. 1930. *The Protestant Ethic and the Spirit of Capitalism.* London: George Allen and Unwin Ltd.

Weinstein, James. 1968. *The Corporate Ideal in the Liberal State.* Boston: Beacon Press.

Wilensky, Harold L. and Charles N. Lebeaux. 1958. *Industrial Society and Social Welfare.* New York: Russell Sage Foundation.

Williams, William. 1961. *The Content of American History.* Cleveland, Ohio: World Publishing Company.

ARTICLES AND PAPERS

Abbott, Edith. 1934. "Abolish the Pauper Laws." *Social Service Review,* VIII, 1–16.

————. 1931. "Backgrounds and Foregrounds in Education for Social Work." *Social Welfare and Professional Education.* Chicago: University of Chicago Press.

————. 1933 and 1935. "Education for Social Work." *Social Work Yearbooks,* Vols. II and III. New York: Russell Sage Foundations.

————. 1936. "Public Welfare in Politics." *Social Service Review,* X, 395–412.

————. 1928. "Some Basic Principles in Professional Education for Social Work." *National Conference of Social Work.*

Addams, Jane. 1911. "The Call of the Social Field." In Alexander Johnson (ed.), *Proceedings of the National Conference of Charities and Correction, Boston, Massachusetts, 1911.* Fort Wayne, Ind.: The Fort Wayne Printing Co.

————. 1899. "A Function of the Social Settlement." *Annals of the American Academy of Political and Social Science,* XIII; quoted in Christopher Lasch (ed.), *The Social Thought of Jane Addams.* Indianapolis: Bobbs-Merrill Co. (1965).

————. 1893. "The Subjective Necessity for Social Settlements." In Jane Addams, *Philanthropy and Social Progress.* New York: Thomas Y. Crowell & Company.

————. 1898. "Why the Ward Boss Rules." *The Outlook,* 58, 6–9.

Allen, Fredrick H. 1933. "Emotional Responses to Economic Change." *Proceedings, National Conference of Social Work, Detroit, 1933,* 333–346.

Anderson, Joseph D. 1982. "Generic and Generalist. Practice and the B.S.W. Curriculum." *Journal of Education for Social Work,* 37–45.

Anon. 1936. "A Glossary for Rank and File: P–S." *Social Work Today,* III, 23.

Anon. 1936. "Should Social Work Employees Use Labor Tactics?—A Symposium." *Social Work Today,* III, 5–7.

Anon. 1938. "Smith Students Organized." *Social Work Today,* VI, 13.

Anon. 1936. "Social Workers and the Presidential Election—A Symposium." *Social Work Today,* IV, 4–7.

Ayres, Phillip W. 1899. "Training for Practical Philanthropy." *American Review of Reviews,* XIX, 205–206.

Baker, Edith. 1935. "How Can Social Case Work Meet Individual Public Relief Clients from the Point of Medical Case Work." *Proceedings, National Conference of Social Work, 1935,* Montreal.

Bancroft, Frank C. 1941. "Philadelphia Story." *Social Work Today,* III, 4–5.

————. 1940. "Social Workers and War: 1917 and 1940." *Social Work Today,* VII, 16–19.

Baldwin, Roger M. 1911. "The Selection and Training of Probation and Attendance Officers." In Alexander Johnson (ed.), *National Conference of Charities and Corrections,* 393–394.

Barnes, Kathleen and Harriet Moore. 1937. "The New Soviet Constitution." *Social Work Today,* IV, 9–10.

Bitterman, Alex and Carel B. Germain. 1979. "Social Work Practice: A Life Model." In Beulah Roberts Compton and Burt Galaway (eds.). *Social Work Processes.* Homewood, Illinois: The Dorsey Press.

Blair, Hector. 1935. "Students Learn." *Social Work Today,* III, 26.

Blum, Arthur and Marvin L. Rosenberg. 1981. "Points and Viewpoints, Washing Dirty Sheets: The Readers' Comments on Social Work." *Social Work*, 26, 524–25.

Borders, Karl. 1933. "Social Workers and a New Social Order." *Proceedings, National Conference of Social Work, 1933, Detroit,* 590–96.

Breckenridge, Sophonisba P. 1934. "Promotion of National and State Legislation by Social Workers." *Proceedings, National Conference of Social Work,* Kansas City.

Bronsin, Henry N. 1948. "Psychiatry Experiments with Selection." *Social Science Review,* XXII, 143.

Bruno, Frank. 1932. "Social Work Objectives in the New Era." *Proceedings, National Conference of Social Work,* Philadelphia, 565–74.

Cahard, J. C. 1937. "Hospices." *Social Work Today,* IV, 25.

Cannon, Antonette. 1933. "Recent Changes in the Philosophy of Social Workers." *National Conference of Social Work,* Detroit.

Chapin, Stuart F. 1919. "The Relations of Sociology and Social Casework." *Proceedings of the National Conference of Social Work,* 358–365.

Cloward, Richard A. and Irwin Epstein. 1967. "Private Social Welfare's Disengagement from the Poor: The Case of Family Adjustment Agencies." In George A. Brazer and Frances P. Purcells (eds.), *Community Action Against Poverty.* New Haven, Connecticut: College and University Press, 40–63.

Cloward, Richard A. and Frances Fox Piven. 1977. "The Acquiescence of Social Work." *Society,* 55–62.

Cohen, Mabel Blake. 1955. "Counter Transference and Anxiety." In Clara Thompson, Milton Mazer and Earl Whitenberg (eds.). *An Outline of Psychoanalysis.* New York: The Modern Library, Random House, 539–564.

Committee on Education and Training, Local 46. 1939. "Union Made Training Program." *Social Work Today,* VI, 6.

Crafts, Rev. William F. 1895. "The New Charity and the Newest." *The Charities Review,* IV, 19–24.

Dallob, Samuel. 1939. "The Schools and the Public Field." *Social Work Today,* VI, 9.

Davies, Stanley P. 1932. "Working toward one professional standard—public and private." *Social Service Review,* VI, 438.

Davison, Arthur. 1936. "Ohio Dodges Responsibility." *Social Work Today,* IV.

Dawes, Anna. 1894. "The Need of Training Schools for a New Profession." *Sociology in Institutions of Learning: Being a Report of the Seventh Section of the International Congress of Charities, Correction, and Philanthropy.* Chicago, 1893, edited by Amos G. Warner. Baltimore: Johns Hopkins Press.

Dexter, Elizabeth. 1935. "Has Case Work a Place in the Administration of Public Relief Proceedings?" *National Conference of Social Work, 1935,* Montreal. Chicago: University of Chicago Press.

Diamond, S. 1936. "Psychoanalysis and Case Work." *Social Work Today,* III, 8–9.

Editorial. 1937. "Appeals for Spain." *Social Work Today,* IV, 4–5.

Editorial. 1936. "Chaos in State Relief." *Social Work Today,* IV, 5.

Editorial. 1940. "Meeting Social Needs: A Peace Program." *Social Work Today*, VII, 5–7.

Editorial. 1942. "The Month—Philadelphia Witch Hunt." *Social Work Today*, IX, 29.

Editorial. 1937. "Running Out on the Unemployed." *Social Work Today*, IV, 3–4.

Editorial. 1936. "Social Work's Stake in the Election." *Social Work Today*, IV, 4.

Editorial. 1938. "Students from Their Ranks." *Social Work Today*, V, 40.

Editorial. 1937. "We Support the President." *Social Work Today*, IV, 3.

Elizabethea, Reginae, Anno xlijj. 1961. "An Act for the Relief of the Poore." In Ralph E. Pumphery and Muriel W. Pumphery. *The Heritage of American Social Work*. New York: Columbia University Press.

Ellis, Peter. 1936. "From the Front Lines, A Letter to Student Social Worker." *Social Work Today*, III, 23–24.

Emerson, Ralph Waldo. 1909. "Self Reliance." *Harvard Classics*, 62. New York: P. F. Collier & Sons Corp.

Erlich, John L. and John E. Tropman. 1974. "Social Work Students, Other Graduate Students, and Issues of Student Protest." *Journal of Education for Social Work*, 10, 22–26.

———. 1969. "The Politics of Participation: Student Power." *Social Work*, 14, 64–72.

Farris, Robert E. 1945. "American Sociology." In George Gurothels and William E. Morse (eds.), *Twentieth Century Sociology*. New York: Philosophical Library.

Fischer, Joel. 1973. "Is Case-Work Effective? A Review." *Social Work*, 18, 5–22.

Fisher, Jacob. 1936. "The Rank and File Movement, 1930–1936." *Social Work Today*, 3, 5–10.

Flexner, Abraham. 1915. "Is Social Work a Profession?" *Proceedings of the National Conference of Charities and Corrections, Baltimore, 1915*. Chicago: Hildemann Printing Co.

Folks, Homer. 1894. "College Graduates in Benevolent Work." In Amos G. Warner (ed.), *Sociology in Institutions of Learning: Being a Report of the Seventh Section of the International Congress of Charities, Corection and Philanthropy, Chicago, 1893*. Baltimore: Johns Hopkins Press.

———. 1933. "Public Relief as a Social Problem." *Proceedings, National Conference of Social Work, 1933*, Detroit.

Frankfurter, Felix. 1915. "Social Work and Professional Training." *Proceedings of the National Conference of Charities and Corrections, Baltimore, 1915*. Chicago: Hildemann Printing Co., 595–596.

Franklin, Benjamin. 1961. "The Life of Benjamin Franklin, Written by Himself." In Pumphery and Pumphery, *The Heritage of American Social Work*. New York: Columbia University Press.

Friedlander, Walter J. 1939. "Social Work Under the Nazi Regime." *Social Work Today*, VII, 9–11.

Fuss, Arthur R. 1937. "WPA After the Election." *Social Work Today,* IV, 3–5.

Gambrill, Eileen, Edwin J. Thomas, and Robert V. Carter. 1971. "Procedure for Socio-Behavioral Practice in Open Settings." *Social Work,* 16, 51–62.

Griscom, John. 1961. "The First Annual Report of the Managers of the Society for the Prevention of Pauperism in the City of New York." In Pumphery and Pumphery, *The Heritage of American Social Work.* New York: Columbia University Press.

Hamilton, Gordon. 1934. "Case Work Responsibility in the Unemployment Relief Agency." *Proceedings, National Conference of Social Work,* Kansas City, 389–398.

Hathway, Marion. 1937. "The Right to Training." *Social Work Today,* V, 11–12.

Herman, Faye. 1936. "Politics in Illinois." *Social Work Today,* IV.

Hodson, William. 1934. "The Social Worker and the New Deal." *National Conference of Social Work, 1934,* Kansas City.

Hoffmann, Zelda. 1935. "Bread into Bullets." *Social Work Today,* IV, 9–10.

Hollis, Florence. 1970. "The Psycho-Social Approach to Casework." In Robert W. Roberts and Robert H. Nee, *Theories of Social Casework.* Chicago: University of Chicago Press.

Jarrett, Mary C. 1919. "The Psychiatric Thread Running Through All Social Work." In *Proceedings of the National Conference of Social Work, 1919.* Chicago: Rogers and Hall, 587–593.

Karpf, Maurice. 1925. "Relation Between Sociology and Social Work." *Journal of Social Forces,* III, 423.

Kerby, Phil. 1967. "Revolt Against the Poor." *The Nation,* 205, 262–267.

Kraft, Ivor. 1969. "The State of the Social Work Profession." In Willard C. Richan (ed.) *Second N.A.S.W. Professional Symposium.* New York: National Association of Social Workers, 343–366.

Kurtz, Russell. 1935. "Social Case Work in a National Program of Social Security." Proceedings, *National Conference of Social Work,* Montreal.

Lee, Porter. 1930. "Social Work: Cause and Function." *Proceedings of the Fifty-Sixth Annual Meeting, 1929 National Conference of Social Work.* Chicago: University of Chicago Press. 3-20.

Lindeman, Eduard C. 1935. "Basic Unities in Social Work." *Proceedings, National Conference of Social Work, 1935,* Montreal.

Litwak, Eugene. 1961. "Models of Bureaucracy which Permit Conflict." *American Journal of Sociology,* 62, 177–184.

Lurie, Harry. 1931. "Review of Changing Psychology in Social Casework by Virginia Robinson." *The Social Service Review,* 5, 488–89.

Lynde, Edward. 1929. "The Significance of Changing Methods in Relief Giving." *The Family,* 8, 135–144.

Mandel, Arch. 1933. "Government Economy and Social Work." *National Proceedings of Social Work, 1933,* Detroit, 456–464.

———. 1932. "What Should We Tell the Public." *Proceedings, National Conference of Social Work, Philadelphia, 1932.*

Marcus, Grace. 1932. "Psychology in Casework." *Proceedings National Conference of Social Work, 1932,* Philadelphia.

Martz, Larry. 1975. "Say Nay Politics." *Newsweek*, 85, 23.

McKinny, Madge. 1939. "The Right of Asylum." *Social Work Today*, VII, 5–6.

McMillan, A. Wayne. 1933. "The Problems of Schools of Social Work." *Proceedings, National Conference of Social Work, 1933*, 631–638.

McMillen, Wayne. 1937. "Trade Unionism for Social Workers." *Social Work Today*, IV, 7–9.

Miller, Henry. 1981. "Dirty Sheets: A Multi-Variant Analysis." *Social Work*, 26, 268–271.

Mills, C. Wright. 1939. "The Professional Ideology of the Social Pathologists." In C. Wright Mills, *Power, Politics, and People*. London: Oxford University Press, 1939.

Morgan, Dwight D. 1934. "Foreign Born and Relief." *Social Work Today*, IV, 11–12.

N.A.S.W. Ad Hoc Committee on Advocacy. 1969. "The Social Worker as Advocate: Champion of Social Victims." *Social Work*, 14, 16–22.

N.A.S.W. 1983. "Membership Survey Shows Practice Shifts." *N.A.S.W. News*, 20, 6–7.

Paulding, J. K. 1895. "Democracy and Charity." *The Charities Review*, IV, 281–290.

Perlman, Helen Harris. 1970. "The Problem Solving Model in Social Casework." In Robert Roberts and Robert Nee, *Theories of Social Casework*. Chicago: University of Chicago Press.

Phillips, John. 1936. "New Jersey Saves Tax Payers Money." *Social Work Today*, IV.

Pinchot, Gifford. 1933. "The Opportunity of Social Work in View of the Trend from Private to Public Relief." *Proceedings National Conference of Social Work, Philadelphia, 1932*. Chicago: University of Chicago Press, 90–96.

Pray, Kenneth L. M. 1942. "The Agency's Role in Service." In Virginia P. Robinson (ed.), *Training for Skill in Social Casework*. Philadelphia: University of Pennsylvania Press, 119.

————. 1934. "Relative Responsibilities of Public and Private Social Work." *National Conference of Social Work, Kansas City*, 204–216.

————. 1947. "When is Community Organization Social Work Practice." *National Conference of Social Welfare Proceedings*, 203–204.

Reed, William J. and Patricia Hanrahan. 1982. "Recent Evaluations of Social Work: Grounds for Optimism." *Social Work*, 328–340.

Reynolds, Bertha. 1931. "A Changing Psychology in Social Case Work." *The Family*, 13, 111–114.

————. 1936. "Education for Public Social Work." *Social Work Today*, III, 10.

Richmond, Mary. 1911. "The Art of Beginning in Social Work." Address given at the National Conference of Charities and Correction, June, 1911.

————. 1896. "Criticism on Reform in Charity." A lecture delivered before the Social Science Club of the Woman's College, Baltimore.

————. 1930. "The Need of a Training School in Applied Philanthropy." A paper read before the National Conference of Charities and Corrections, 1987, in Joanna C. Colcord and Ruth Z. S. Mann, *The Long View: Papers and Addresses by Mary E. Richmond.* New York: Russell Sage Foundation, 1930, 99–104.

———. 1905. "The Retail Method of Reform." An address given before the Ethical Cultural Society of Philadelphia. April 17, 1905.

———. 1930. "The Settlement and Friendly Visiting." In Joanna C. Colcord and Ruth Z. S. Mann, (eds.), *The Long View, Papers and Addresses by Mary Richmond.* New York: Russell Sage Foundation, 1930, 121–122.

———. 1911. "The Art of Beginning in Social Work." Address given at the National Conference of Charities and Correction, June, 1911.

———. 1930. "The Training of Charity Workers." A paper read at the meeting of the Civic Club, Philadelphia March 19, 1897, in Joanna C. Colcord and Ruth Z. S. Mann, (eds.), *The Long View Papers and Addresses by Mary Richmond.* New York: Russell Sage Foundation, 1930, 90.

Robinson, Virginia. "The Meaning of Skill." In Virginia Robinson (ed.). *Training for Skill in Social Casework.* Philadelphia: University of Pennsylvania Press, 1942, 7–31.

Rosenfeld, Kurt. 1935. "In the Lion's Mouth." *Social Work Today,* III, 18–19.

Rothman, Jack. 1970. "Three Models of Community Organization Practice." In Fred M. Cox, John L. Ehrlich, Jack Rothman, and John E. Tropman. *Strategies of Community Organization.* Itasca, Ill.: F. E. Peacock, Publishers, 20–36.

Schlauch, Margaret. 1935. "On the Brink, War and Fascism Today." *Social Work Today,* III, 14–15.

Schubert, Margaret. 1969. "Making the Best Use of Traditional and Atypical Field Placements." In Betty Lacey Jones (ed.), *Current Patterns in Field Instruction in Graduate Social Work Education.* New York: Council on Social Work Education, 3–11.

Scott, W. Richard. 1969. "Professional Employees in a Bureaucratic Structure; Social Work." In Amitai Etzioni (ed.), *The Semi-Professionals and Their Organization.* New York: The Free Press, 131–134.

Selver, William C. "View from Capitol Hill: Harrassment and Survival." In James L. Sundquist (ed.) *On Fighting Poverty: Perspectives from Experience.* New York: Basic Books, 166.

Simon, Bernice K. 1970. "Social Casework Therapy: An Overview." In Robert W. Roberts and Robert H. Nee, *Theories of Social Casework.* Chicago: University of Chicago Press, 378.

Simpson, Herbert. 1934. "Taxation and Its Implications for Social Work." *Proceedings National Conference of Social Work,* 1934, Kansas City.

Siporin, Max. 1981. "Review of Social work Practice: A Radical Perspective by Jeffrey Galper." *Social Work,* 26, 520.

Smalley, Ruth. 1970. "The Functional Approach to Casework." In Robert Roberts and Robert Nee (eds.), *Theories of Social Casework.* Chicago: University of Chicago Press, 1970, 80–81.

Smith, Zilpha. 1892. "The Education of the Friendly Visitor." *Proceedings of the National Conference of Charities and Correction.* Boston: Press of George H. Ellis, 1892, 445.

Specht, Harry. 1972. "The Deprofessionalization of Social Work." *Social Work,* 17, 3–15.

———. 1967. "Disruptive Tactics." *Social Work,* 14, 5–15.

Stein, Herman D. 1969. "Reflections on Competence and Competence and Ideology in Social Work Education." *Proceedings of Education for Social Work,* 5.

Stillman, Charles C. 1932. "A Social Work Education Program." *Proceedings, National Conference of Social Work,* Philadelphia, 1932.

Szyz, Florence. 1931. "Letter." *The Family,* 13, 197–99.

———. 1936. "Relation of a Standard of Educational Training to Professional Practice." *Proceedings, National Conference of Social Work,* 1936, 103.

Taylor, Graham. 1894. "Sociology in Theological Seminaries." In Amos Warner (ed.), *Sociology in Institutions of Higher Learning, Being a Report of the Seventh Section of the International Congress of Charities, Correction and Philanthropy,* Chicago, June 1893. Baltimore: The Johns Hopkins Press, 65.

Thomas, Edwin. 1970. "Behavior Modification and Casework." In Robert Roberts and Robert Nee (eds.), *Theories of Social Casework.* Chicago: University of Chicago Press, 1970, 181–218.

———. 1968. "Selected Socio-Behavioral Techniques and Principles: An Approach to Interpersonal Helping." *Social Work,* 13, 12.

Van Kleeck, Mary. 1934. "Common Goals of Labor and Social Work." *Proceedings, National Conference of Social Work,* 1934, 284–303.

Van Kleeck, Mary. 1940. "Social Work in the World Crisis." *Social Work Today,* VII, 5–8.

Van Kleeck, Mary. 1935. "Sources of Power for the Social Work Program—Do We Need a Labor Party." *Social Work Today,* III, 8–11.

Warner, Amos. 1961. "Notes on the Statistical Determination of the Causes of Poverty." Publications of the American Statistical Association. New Series I, No. 5 (1889), 188–201. In Ralph E. Pumphrey and Muriel W. Pumphrey, *The Heritage of American Social Work.* New York: Columbia University Press, 240–41.

———. 1894. "Philanthropy in Educational Institutions." In Amos Warner, *Sociology in Institutions of Learning.* Baltimore: The Johns Hopkins Press, 1894, 80–92.

Yelaja, Shankar A. "Functional Theory for Social Work Practice." In Francis J. Turner (ed.), *Social Work Treatment: Interlocking Theoretical Approaches.* Second Edition; New York: The Free Press, 1979, 123–143.

UNPUBLISHED MATERIALS

Broadhurst, Betty Page. 1971. "Social Thought, Social Practice, and Social Work Education: Sanborn, Ely, Warner, Richmond." Unpublished doctoral dissertation, School of Social Work, Columbia University.

Falk, Ursula. 1974. "History of the Development of Social Work in the United States." Unpublished doctoral dissertation, University of Buffalo.

Hellenbrand, Shirley C. 1965. "Main Currents in Social Casework, 1918–1936: The Development of Social Casework in the United States as Reflected in the Literature and in Classroom Teaching Materials." Unpublished doctoral dissertation, School of Social Work, Columbia University.

Lunt, Sally Herman. "The Professionalization of Social Work, with Special Reference to the School for Social Workers (Boston 1904)." Unpublished doctoral dissertation, Harvard University.

Index